The Wilding of America

Greed, Violence, and the
New American Dream

Contemporary Social Issues

George Ritzer, *Series Editor*

Urban Enclaves: Identity and Place in America
Mark Abrahamson, *University of Connecticut*

Just Revenge: Costs and Consequences of the Death Penalty
Mark Costanzo, *Claremont McKenna College*

The Wilding of America: Greed, Violence, and the New American Dream
Charles Derber, *Boston College*

Between Politics and Reason: The Drug Legalization Debate
Erich Goode, *State University of New York, Stony Brook*

The Culture of Surveillance: Discipline and Social Control in the United States
William G. Staples, *University of Kansas*

The Myth of Self-Esteem
John P. Hewitt, *University of Massachusetts, Amherst*

FORTHCOMING

Sexual Saturation
Kenneth Kammeyer, *University of Maryland, Baltimore*

Contemporary Social Issues
Series Editor: George Ritzer, *University of Maryland*

The Wilding of America

America

Greed, Violence, and the New American Dream

Second Edition

Charles Derber
Boston College

Worth Publishers

The Wilding of America, Second Edition

Printed in the United States of America.

ISBN: 0-7167-5321-9

First printing, 2001

Sponsoring Editor: Laura J. Edwards
Marketing Manager: JoEllen Tomlinson
Associate Managing Editor: Tracey Kuehn
Production Manager: Barbara Anne Seixas
Art Director: Barbara Reingold
Text Designer: Lissi Sigillo
Composition: Matrix Publishing Services
Printing and Binding: R. R. Donnelley & Sons Company

Cover art: V.C.L./Chris Ryan/FPG

Library of Congress Cataloging-in-Publication Data
Derber, Charles.
    The wilding of America : how greed and violence are eroding our nation's character /
Charles Derber.
        p. cm. — (Contemporary social issues)
    Includes bibliographical references and index.
    I. Violence—United States. 2. Violent crimes—United States. 3. Wealth—Moral and
ethical aspects—United States. 4. United States—Social conditions—1980– I. Title II.
Contemporary social issues (New York, N.Y.)

HN90.V5.D47 2001
303.6'0973—dc21

                                                                    2001026730

Worth Publishers
41 Madison Avenue
New York, New York 10010
www.worthpublishers.com

To Elena—For rekindling my faith in America and in myself

To my parents, Milton and Zelda Derber—For standing by me from the beginning and never letting me down

And to Morrie Schwartz—For giving me the gift of his life-sustaining unconditional love to the very end

Contents

Foreword

As we move into the twenty-first century, we confront a seemingly endless array of pressing social issues: crime, urban decay, inequality, ecological threats, rampant consumerism, war, AIDS, inadequate health care, national and personal debt, and many more. Although such problems are regularly dealt with in newspapers, magazines, and trade books and on radio and television, such popular treatment has severe limitations. By examining these issues systematically through the lens of sociology, we can gain greater insight into them and be better able to deal with them. It was to this end that St. Martin's Press created this series on contemporary social issues, and Worth Publishers has chosen to continue it.

Each book in the series casts a new and distinctive light on a familiar social issue, while challenging the conventional view, which may obscure as much as it clarifies. Phenomena that seem disparate and unrelated are shown to have many commonalities and to reflect a major, but often unrecognized, trend within the larger society. Or a systematic comparative investigation demonstrates the existence of social causes or consequences that are overlooked by other types of analysis. In uncovering such realities the books in this series are much more than intellectual exercises; they have powerful practical implications for our lives and for the structure of society.

At another level, this series fills a void in book publishing. There is certainly no shortage of academic titles, but those books tend to be introductory texts for undergraduates or advanced monographs for professional scholars. Missing are broadly accessible, issue-oriented books appropriate for all students (and for general readers). The books in this series occupy that niche somewhere between popular trade books and monographs. Like trade books, they deal with important and interesting social issues, are well written, and are as jargon free as possible. However, they are more rigorous than trade books in meeting academic standards for writing and research. Although they are not textbooks, they often explore topics covered in basic textbooks and therefore are easily integrated into the curriculum of sociology and other disciplines.

Each of the books in the "Contemporary Social Issues" series is a new and distinctive piece of work. I believe that students, serious general readers, and professors will all find the books to be informative, interesting, thought provoking, and exciting.

—*George Ritzer*

Preface

In 1992, after publishing the first edition of this book, I went to New York City to talk about "wilding" on WABC, the flagship radio station of ABC. The station invited me shortly after the brutal Central Park gang-rape of a jogger—the event that led the media to coin the term *wilding*. Although I hoped to educate New Yorkers, it turned out that the Big Apple still had a few things to teach me about my subject.

As I was waiting in the studio for my turn, I heard my talk-show host, Bob Grant, talk about the city's graffiti problem and raise one possible solution: cutting off the hands of the young offenders. I sensed I had some differences with this tough hombre, but I realized why he had invited me down. He and his callers were obsessed with the disintegration of the city and young wilders running loose on the street.

I soon learned why, in a very personal way. The day after my conversation with Grant, I drove down at noon to a conference on the lower West Side of Manhattan. After about an hour, I had a premonition that I had better check my car, probably a residue of my conversation with Grant. I walked quickly back to the street and could hardly believe my eyes. My new Honda Accord was sitting only on its naked brake drums—tires, rims, and lug nuts all stripped. In the wink of an eye, my car had been transformed into one of those abandoned vehicles one sees in deserted areas of the South Bronx, except that the windows were not broken or the inside looted.

It was early Saturday afternoon with lots of people around. In a state of disbelief, I ran up to two policemen, who had just arrived at the corner to write up an unrelated accident. They told me to wait, and in the next fifteen minutes, I watched a parade of people drive up to my car, stop, get out, and survey my vehicle. I quickly recognized that they were interested in finishing the job: the radio, the carburetor, anything to sell.

While I pleaded with the police to help me tow the car to a garage before it was picked clean, they shrugged their shoulders and told me they could not tow it unless I had committed a crime in it. I was lucky enough to find a garage, a tow truck, and a tire shop. The tire-shop proprietor, who told me his own car had disappeared from in front of his house in the Bronx, sounded just like Bob Grant and his callers. He wanted to know if my home state of Massachusetts had a death penalty. When I mentioned

I was a teacher, he said he figured kids today were becoming a generation of criminals and needed a moral education more than technical skills. As I drove off, he waved and yelled out, "Please help us raise a better generation."

His plea helps to define the mission of this book. As we move into the new century, the national crises of violence and greed that motivated my desire to write this book have deepened. I have written this new edition to show how new conditions cry out for a new understanding and urgent new responses. Americans, although deluged with stories of crime and corruption, are not making the connections necessary to explain the real nature of the wilding problem or what might solve it.

The media publicize sensational street violence and personal crimes that sell tabloids or TV advertising. But wilding, as viewed by a sociologist, involves multiple forms of violence, including that perpetrated in the corporate suites as well as on the streets. Only a few media stories suggest that the criminals in the corporate boardrooms and on the street share elements of the same greed and the same dream.

Street wilding and white-collar wilding are racing out of control at the same time, reflecting new contradictions between today's American Dream and American prospects for success. Americans pursue divisive and increasingly unattainable goals that cannot meet our deepest needs for respect, love, and justice. As the Dream simultaneously beckons and recedes, the price of failure is frustration and rage; the price of success, too often, is inner emptiness and a debilitating fear of those left behind. Deepening inequalities, rising tides of social frustration, and corrosive moral decay threaten the bonds of community and the very survival of the social fabric.

For the citizen, this is frightening, but for the sociologist the fear inspires a sense of burning intellectual mission. The impending sense of social breakdown raises a central question: What makes community—and society itself—possible at all? This is the core problem of sociology, one with special urgency for our highly individualistic and competitive capitalist societies, but it is not a problem for sociologists alone.

The metaphor of societal illness that the wilding epidemic evokes points to the need for all of us to become practitioners of the art of social healing. This book offers one diagnosis of our weakened but still resilient collective condition. My hope is that the cure cannot long resist an awakened community brave enough to look deeply at its shared pathologies and empowered with the insights of the sociological imagination.

Acknowledgments

I am grateful to many friends and colleagues whose excitement about this book helped it come to fruition. David Karp's enthusiasm at early stages nourished my own belief in the project, and his continuing close reading of the manuscript helped me improve the book at every stage. Morrie Schwartz spurred me on with his insights and always generous emotional support. I thank Noam Chomsky, Jonathan Kozol, Howard Zinn, Robert Reich, Robert Coles, Philip Slater, Ann Cordilia, and Alvin Poussaint for reading the manuscript and responding to it. I am also grateful to my colleagues Ritchie Lowry, Severyn Bruyn, David Horton Smith, Mike Malec, and Paul Gray for helpful suggestions, and especially to John Williamson and S. M. (Mike) Miller for their support and many useful ideas.

I want to thank George Ritzer who gave me strong encouragement to write this edition. I also want to thank Laura Edwards, Tracey Kuehn, and Barbara Seixas for their help in producing this new edition.

I owe much to my parents, who nurtured the concern for society that animates this book. And also to Elena Kolesnikova, who heroically endured the obsessions of an author about his work. She contributed ideas, helped me overcome my doubts, and nourished me along the way.

The Good Man Fills His Own Stomach

All-American Crimes and Misdemeanors

The readings of history and anthropology . . . give us no reason to believe that societies have built-in self preservative systems.

—Margaret Mead

Wilding in Black and White

"All day I got grabbed," said Yaneira Davis, 20, a Rutgers student. She was describing her bad Sunday—Puerto Rican Day, on June 11, 2000, in New York City's Central Park. "The attitude was," Yaneira continued, "'I'm going to touch you, and I don't care what you say.'" Ashana Cover and Josina Lawrence, both 21, who were also in Central Park that day, said that they were sprayed, groped, and had their tops pulled off. Stephanie, who did not want her last name used, said that 20 guys "were coming at me from all directions, and they were grabbing my butt, groping my butt, and I was screaming and I was trying to get through, trying to get away." Twenty-seven other women reported that groups of young men stripped them, groped their breasts and genitals, and robbed them of jewelry and purses.[1]

Videotapes captured the scene, beamed around the world by satellite TV. While onlookers, including police, watched passively or with some amusement, the young victims ran in terror, trying to keep their clothes from being torn off and often screaming hysterically. The young men, many drunk or stoned, seemed to be greatly enjoying themselves, going from one woman to another and yelping with pleasure as they ogled, chased, stripped, and groped their prey.[2]

Police estimate that at least 200 men were involved and scores of women assaulted and sexually abused. The violence had begun during prefestivities the night before as the young men, according to one of their lawyers, "were there chillin', smokin' a couple cigarettes and watchin' the babes go by." They escalated the violence in broad daylight, inflicting mayhem throughout the entire day of celebration and into the evening. Scores of men were eventually arrested, although some of the victims filed suit against police for doing nothing to protect them.[3]

The graphic videotapes catapulted the event into the headlines and provoked debate everywhere about violence in America. Media pundits called the gangs of young men a "wolfpack" that felt free to commit unusually savage acts in full public view. Journalists agreed that this was another outbreak of "wilding," reminding readers of a terrifying crime that had gripped the nation 11 years earlier. We have to return to that event if we want to understand how the term *wilding* entered our culture to become a symbol of one of America's deepest social crises.

On April 19, 1989, in New York City, a group of teenagers aged 14 to 16 went into Central Park, ironically the very same site as the Puerto Rican Day disaster. It was a clear night and not too cold, at least not too cold to discourage hardy joggers from getting their exercise. The teenagers dispersed into small bands and began targeting victims for some mischief. One group of six youths came upon a young woman jogging alone past a grove of sycamore trees. They cornered her in a gully and began to have some "fun."

That fun would also capture headlines around the world. Using rocks, knives, and a metal pipe, they attacked her. Some pinned her down while others beat and raped her. One defendant, Kharey Wise, aged 17, told police that he held the jogger's legs while a friend repeatedly cut her with a knife. They then smashed her with a rock and punched her face, Wise said, until she "stopped moving." After half an hour, she had lost three-quarters of her blood and was unconscious. The group left her for dead.[4]

What most captured public attention were the spirits of the assaulters during and after their crime. According to 15-year-old Kevin Richardson, one of the participants, "Everyone laughed and was leaping around." One youth was quoted by police as saying, "It was fun . . . something to do." Asked if they felt pretty good about what they had done, Richardson said "yes." Police reported a sense of "smugness" and "no remorse" among the youths.[5]

From this event, a new word was born: *wilding.* According to press reports, it was the term the youths themselves used to describe their behavior—and it seemed appropriate. The savagery of the crime, which left the victim brain-damaged and in a coma for weeks, evoked the image of a predatory lion in the bush mangling its helpless prey. Equally shocking was the blasé attitude of the attackers. It had been no big deal, a source of temporary gratification and amusement. They were "mindless marauders seeking a thrill," said Judge Thomas B. Galligan of Manhattan, who sentenced three of the teenagers to a maximum term of 5 to 10 years, charging them with turning Central Park into a "torture chamber." These were youths who seemed stripped of the emotional veneer of civilized humans, creatures of a wilderness where anything goes.[6]

The story quickly became tied to the race and class of the predators and their prey. The youths were black and from the inner city, although from stable working families. The victim was white, with degrees from Wellesley and Yale, and a wealthy 28-year-old executive at Salomon Brothers, one of the great firms of Wall Street.

To white middle-class Americans, wilding symbolized something real and terrifying about life in the United States. Things were falling apart, at least in the hearts of America's major cities. Most suburbanites did not feel their own neighborhoods had become wild, but they could not imagine walking into Central Park at night. Drugs, crime, and unemployment had made the inner city wild.

The fear of wilding became fear of the Other: those locked out of the American Dream. They had not yet invaded the world most Americans felt part of, but they menaced it. The Central Park attack made the threat real, and it unleashed fear among the general population and a backlash of rage among politicians and other public figures. Mayor Edward Koch called for the death penalty. Donald Trump took out ads in four newspapers, writing "I want to hate these murderers . . . I want them to be afraid." Trump told *Newsweek* that he "had gotten hundreds and hundreds of letters of support."[7]

Six months later, a second remarkably vicious crime grabbed people's attention all over the country. On October 23, 1989, Charles and Carol Stuart left a birthing class at Boston's Brigham and Women's Hospital, walked to their car parked in the adjoining Mission Hill neighborhood, and got in. Within minutes, Carol Stuart, eight-months pregnant, was dead, shot point-blank in the head. Her husband, a stunned nation would learn from police accounts two months later, was her assassin. He had allegedly killed her to collect hundreds of thousands of dollars in life insurance money and open a restaurant. Opening a restaurant, Americans everywhere learned, had long been Charles Stuart's American Dream.

Many white middle-class Americans seemed instinctively to believe Stuart's story when he told police that a black gunman shot him and his wife, leaving Carol Stuart dead and Stuart himself with a severe bullet wound in the abdomen. When Stuart's brother Matthew went to the police to tell them of Charles's involvement, and when Charles Stuart subsequently apparently committed suicide by jumping off the Tobin Bridge into the river bearing his given name, some of the threads connecting his crime to the horrible rape in Central Park began to emerge. Stuart had duped a whole nation by playing on the fear of the wild Other. Aware of the vivid images of gangs of black youths rampaging through dark city streets, Stuart brilliantly concocted a story that would resonate with white Americans' deepest anxieties. Dr. Alvin Poussaint, Harvard professor and adviser to Bill Cosby, said, "Stuart had all the ingredients. . . . [H]e gave blacks a killer image and put himself in the role of a model, an ideal Camelot type that white people could identify with."[8]

Charles Stuart's crime became a national obsession. A 21-year-old Oklahoman visiting Boston told a *Boston Globe* reporter, "You wouldn't believe the attention this is getting back home. It's all anyone can talk about. I've taken more pictures of this fur shop and Stuart's house than any of the stuff you're supposed to take pictures of in Boston."[9] The quiet Stuart block in Reading had become what the *Globe* called a "macabre mecca," with hundreds of cars, full of the curious and the perplexed, parked or passing by. One reason may have been that white middle-class Americans everywhere had an uncomfortable sense that, as the 1990s began, the Stuart case was telling them something about themselves. Stuart, after all, was living the American Dream and reaping its benefits—a tall, dark, athletic man with roots in working-class Revere making more than $100,000 a year selling fur coats, married to a lovely, adoring wife, and living the good life in suburban Reading, complete with swimming pool. Had the American Dream itself become the progenitor of a kind of wilding? Was it possible that not only the inner cities of America but also its comfortable suburbs were becoming wild places? Could "white wilding" be as serious a problem as the "black wilding" publicized in the mass media? Was America at the turn of the decade becoming a wilding society?

To answer these questions we have to look far beyond such exceptional events as the Central Park rape and the Stuart murder. We shall see that there are many less extreme forms of wilding, including a wide range of antisocial acts that are neither criminal nor physically violent. Wilding includes the ordinary as well as the extraordinary, may be profit-oriented or pleasure-seeking, and can infect corporations and governments as well as individuals of every race, class, and gender.

The Mountain People: A Wilding Culture

Between 1964 and 1967, anthropologist Colin Turnbull lived among the people of Uganda known as the Ik, an unfortunate people expelled by an uncaring government from their traditional hunting lands to extremely barren mountainous areas. In 1972, Turnbull published a haunting book about his experiences that left no doubt that a whole society can embrace wilding as a way of life.[10]

When Turnbull first came to the Ik, he met Atum, a sprightly, bare-foot old man with a sweet smile, who helped guide Turnbull to remote Ik villages. Atum warned Turnbull right away that everyone would ask for food. Although many would indeed be hungry, he said, most could fend for themselves, and their pleas should not be trusted; Turnbull, Atum stressed, should on no account give them anything. But before Atum left that day, he mentioned that his own wife was severely ill and desperately needed food and medicine. On reaching his village, Atum told Turnbull his wife was too sick to come out. Later, Turnbull heard exchanges between Atum and his sick wife, as well as her moans, which were wrenching. When Atum pleaded for help, Turnbull gave him food and some aspirin.

Some weeks later, Atum stepped up his requests for food and medicine, saying his wife was getting sicker. Turnbull was not seriously concerned, urging Atum to get her to a hospital. Atum refused, saying "she wasn't that sick." Shortly thereafter, Atum's brother-in-law came to Turnbull and told him that Atum was selling the medicine that Turnbull had been giving him for his wife. Turnbull, not terribly surprised, said that "that was too bad for his wife." The brother-in-law, enjoying the joke enormously, finally explained that Atum's wife "had been dead for weeks" and that Atum had "burned her inside the compound so you wouldn't know." No wonder Atum had not wanted his wife to go the hospital, Turnbull thought to himself: "She was worth far more to him dead than alive."[11]

Startling to Turnbull was not only the immense glee the brother-in-law seemed to take in the "joke" inflicted on his dying sister, but the utter lack of embarrassment Atum showed when confronted with his lie. Atum shrugged it off, showing no remorse whatsoever, saying he had simply forgotten to tell Turnbull. That his little business enterprise may have led to his wife's death was the last thing on Atum's mind. This was one of the first of many events that made Turnbull wonder whether there was any limit to what an Ik would do to get food and money.

Some time later, Turnbull came across Lomeja, an Ik man he had met much earlier. Lomeja had been shot during an attack by neighboring tribesmen and was lying in a pool of his own blood, apparently dying from two bullet wounds in the stomach. Still alive and conscious, Lomeja looked up at Turnbull and asked for some tea. Shaken, Turnbull returned to his Land Rover and filled a big, new, yellow enamel mug. When he returned, Lomeja's wife was bending over her husband. She was trying to "fold him up" in the dead position, although he was not yet dead, and started shrieking at Turnbull to leave Lomeja alone because he was already dead. Lomeja found the strength to resist his wife's premature efforts to bury him and was trying to push her aside. Turnbull managed to get the cup of tea to Lomeja, who was still strong enough to reach out for it and sip it. Suddenly, Turnbull heard a loud giggle and saw Lomeja's sister, Kimat. Attracted by all the yelling, she had "seen that lovely new, bright yellow enamel mug of hot, sweet tea, had snatched it from her brother's face and made off with it, proud and joyful. She not only had the tea, she also had the mug. She drank as she ran, laughing and delighted at herself."[12]

Turnbull came to describe the Ik as "the loveless people." Each Ik valued only his or her own survival, regarding everyone else as a competitor for food. Ik life had become a grim process of trying to find enough food to stay alive each day. The hunt consumed all their resources, leaving virtually no reserve for feelings of any kind, nor for any moral scruples that might interfere with filling their stomachs. As Margaret Mead wrote, the Ik had become "a people who have become monstrous beyond belief." Scientist Ashley Montagu wrote that the Ik are "a people who are dying because they have abandoned their own humanity."[13]

Ik families elevated wilding to a high art. Turnbull met Adupa, a young girl of perhaps 6, who was so malnourished that her stomach was grossly distended and her legs and arms spindly. Her parents had decided she had become a liability and threw her out of their hut. Because she was now too weak to go out on long scavenging ventures, as did the other children, she would wander as far as her strength would allow, pick up scraps of bone or half-eaten berries, and then come back to her parents' place, waiting to be brought back in. Days later, her parents, tiring of her crying, finally brought her in and promised to feed her. Adupa was happy and stopped crying. The parents went out and "closed the asak behind them, so tight that weak little Adupa could never have moved it if she had tried."[14] Adupa waited for them to come back with the food they had promised, but they did not return until an entire week had passed, when they knew Adupa would be dead. Adupa's parents took her rotting remains, Turnbull writes, and threw them out "as one does the riper garbage, a good distance away." There was no burial—and no tears.[15]

Both morality and personality among the Ik were dedicated to the single all-consuming passion for self-preservation. There was simply "not room in the life of these people," Turnbull observes dryly, "for such luxuries as family and sentiment and love." Nor for any morality beyond "marangik," the new Ik concept of goodness, which means filling one's own stomach.

The Ik in Us

Long before the rape in Central Park or the Stuart murder, Ashley Montagu, commenting on Turnbull's work, wrote that "the parallel with our own society is deadly." In 1972, when Turnbull published his book, wilding had not become part of the American vocabulary, nor did Americans yet face declining living standards, let alone the kind of starvation experienced by the Ik. Americans were obviously not killing their parents or children for money, but they dedicated themselves to self-interested pursuits with a passion not unlike that of the Ik.

In America, a land of plenty, there was the luxury of a rhetoric of morality and feelings of empathy and love. But wasn't the American Dream a paean to individualistic enterprise, and couldn't such enterprise be conceived in some of the same unsentimental metaphors used by Turnbull about the Ik? The Ik community, he writes, "reveals itself for what it is, a conglomeration of individuals of all ages, each going his own way in search of food and water, like a plague of locusts spread over the land."[16]

America now faces a wilding epidemic that is eating at the country's social foundation and could rot it. The American case is much less advanced than the Ik's, but the disease is deeply rooted and is spreading throughout the political leadership, the business community, and the general population. Strong medicine can turn the situation around, but if we fail to act now, the epidemic could prove irreversible.

8

Only a handful of Americans are "ultimate wilders" like Charles Stuart. Such killers are noteworthy mainly because they may help wake us to the wilding plague spreading among thousands of less extreme wilders who are not killers. Wilding includes a vast spectrum of self-centered and self-aggrandizing behavior that harms others. A wilding epidemic tears at the social fabric and threatens to unravel society itself, ultimately reflecting the erosion of the moral order and the withdrawal of feelings and commitments from others to oneself, to "number one."

The wilding virus comes in radically different strains. There is *expressive wilding*: wilding for the sheer satisfaction of indulging one's own destructive impulses, the kind found among both groups of Central Park young men and the growing number of American youth who heave rocks off highway overpasses in the hope of smashing the windshields of unknown drivers passing innocently below. The hockey and soccer fathers who attack coaches or other parents are other expressive wilders, as are drivers engaging in road rage. Road rage has reached such epidemic proportions—as has workplace rage, school rage, and air rage—that leading pundits now talk of "dies irae," or America's day of rage. The country's most famous perpetrator is O. J. Simpson, who acted out the domestic violence that is one of the most common and Ik-like forms of expressive wilding. His alleged repeated abuse of his wife to sate his jealousy, maintain his control, or simply gratify his emotions of the moment raises serious questions about the nightmarish spread of family violence among rich and poor alike. The national obsession with Simpson reflects the fear that when a country's icon beats his wife black and blue, smashes her car's windshield with a baseball bat, stalks her, and is finally charged with her murder—of which a jury acquitted him in a controversial verdict—we all participate in the crime, for heroes act out the passions and values of the cultures that lionize them.

Although mainly an example of expressive wilding—in 2001 he was arrested for road rage violence—O. J. has also modeled *instrumental wilding*. Not simply for fun or purely emotive gratification, this is wilding for money, career advancement, or other calculable personal gain. Simpson began as a youngster, running with gangs that stole food. Fantastically ambitious and opportunistic, he later took naturally to a life of single-minded corporate salesmanship, obsessively remaking his voice, wardrobe, and demeanor according to the image lessons of the Hertz ad executives who greased his career; wheeling and dealing to sign movie deals and buy companies such as the Pioneer Chicken franchise (destroyed in the 1992 LA riots); and eventually succumbing to the greed-soaked financial dealings that led him, along with other entrepreneurial high-rollers of his era, to bad loans and collapsed business deals.

Most instrumental wilding is far less dramatic or bizarre, involving garden varieties of ambition, competitiveness, careerism, and greed that advance the self at the cost of others. Expressive and instrumental wilding have in common an antisocial self-centeredness made possible by a stunning collapse of moral restraints and a chilling lack of empathy. I am mainly concerned in this book with instrumental wilding because it is the form most intimately connected with the American Dream and least understood in its poisonous effects on society.[17]

Although much wilding is criminal, there is a vast spectrum of perfectly legal wilding, exemplified by the careerist who indifferently betrays or steps on colleagues to advance up the ladder. There are forms of wilding, such as lying and cheating, that are officially discouraged, but others, such as the frantic and single-minded pursuit of wealth, are cultivated by some of the country's leading corporations and financial institutions. Likewise, there are important differences in the severity of wilding behaviors; killing a spouse for money is obviously far more brutal than stealing a wallet or cheating on an exam. But there are distinct types and degrees of infection in any affliction, ranging from terminal cases such as Stuart, to intermediate cases such as the savings-and-loan crooks, to those who are either petty wilders or rarely exhibit symptoms at all. The latter categories include large numbers of Americans who may struggle internally with their wilding impulses but remain healthy enough to restrain them. The variation is similar to that in heart disease; those with only partial clogging of their arteries and no symptoms are, indeed, different from those with full-blown, advanced arteriosclerosis, and those least afflicted may never develop the terminal stage of the illness. But these differences are normally ones of degree rather than of kind; the same underlying pathology—whether embryonic or full-blown—is at work among people with mild and severe cases.

There are, nonetheless, real differences between white lies or misdemeanors (forms of petty wilding) and serious wilding of the Central Park or Charles Stuart variety. Petty wilding occurs in all cultures, will persist as long as most people are not saints, and in limited doses does not necessarily threaten civil order. When so limited as not to constitute a grave social danger, it might better be described as "incipient wilding" and is not of concern here.

However, certain types of petty wildings are growing at an alarming rate in America, as I document in Chapter 3 in my discussion of minor lying, cheating, and ordinary competitiveness with and indifference to others. Such transgressions on an epidemic scale can reach a critical mass and become as serious a threat to society as violent crime or huge investment scams on Wall Street. It is not the degree of brutality or violence but the consequence for society that ultimately matters, and I thus consider the full spectrum of wilding acts—from petty to outrageous—that together constitute a clear and present danger to America's social fabric.

Three Types of Wilding: Economic, Political, and Social

Wilding, sociologically conceived, extends far beyond random violence by youth gangs, the current media definition, to include three types of assault on society. *Economic wilding* is the morally uninhibited pursuit of money by individuals or businesses at the expense of others. *Political wilding* is the abuse of political office to benefit oneself or one's own social class, or the wielding of political authority to inflict morally unacceptable suffering on citizens at home or abroad. *Social wilding* ranges from personal or family acts of violence, such as child or spouse abuse, to collective forms of selfishness that weaken society, such as affluent suburbs turning their backs on bleeding central cities.

Economic wilders include convicted billionaire financier Michael Milken as well as indicted billionaire Marc Rich (the latter pardoned by President Clinton in 2001 after Rich's wife donated hundreds of thousands of dollars to the Democratic party and Clinton's presidential library). Economic wilders are a different species from the Central Park perpetrators, since they wild for money rather than for fun or sex. Milken was indicted on 98 counts of racketeering and jailed after confessing to six major financial crimes, while Rich escaped to Europe after being indicted for tax evasion, wire fraud, and racketeering. Partly because of differing opportunities and incentives, people wild in different ways and for exceedingly varied reasons and motives ranging from greed and lust to getting attention or respect. The different forms of wilding, however, are all manifestations of degraded American individualism.

Wilding is individualism run amok, and the wilding epidemic is the face of America's individualistic culture in an advanced state of disrepair. Individualistic culture promotes the freedom of the individual and in its healthy form nurtures human development and individual rights. In its degraded form, it becomes a license for unrestrained and sociopathic self-interest.

Wilding and Not Wilding: Varieties of Individualism

Wilding—a degenerate form of individualism—encompasses a huge variety of antisocial behavior. It includes so many seemingly unrelated acts that it might appear to stand for everything—or nothing. But wilding includes only a small subset of the entire range of behaviors that sociologists describe as *individualistic*, a term that arguably can be applied to any self-interested behavior. In a society such as that of the United States, dominated by individualistic values and a market system that rewards self-interest, some might argue that virtually all socially prescribed behavior has an individualistic dimension.

I propose a far more restrictive definition of *wilding*. Not all individualistic behavior is wilding, nor is wilding an umbrella term for any form of self-interested or "bad" behavior. As noted earlier, wilding refers to self-oriented behavior that hurts others and damages the social fabric, and this excludes many types of individualistic action. The Jewish sage Hillel wrote, "If I am for myself alone, what am I?" Yet this quote begins, "If I am not for myself, who will be for me?" His maxim suggests that many forms of self-interest are necessary and contribute to the well-being of others.

A doctor who works hard to perfect her medical skills may advance her own career, but she also saves lives. A superbly conditioned professional athlete may enrich himself by his competitiveness or ambition, but he also entertains and gives pleasure to his fans. If I strive to be the best writer I can be—an individualistic aspiration—I am educating others while fulfilling myself. In none of these cases is individualistic behavior itself necessarily wilding. Actions that advance one's own interests and either help or do not harm others are not forms of wilding, even when motivated by competitiveness or acquisitiveness.

Wilding includes only individualistic behavior that advances or indulges the self by hurting others. If the doctor advances her skills and career by cheating on tests, trampling on her colleagues, or using her patients as guinea pigs, her self-interest has degraded into wilding. The athlete who illicitly uses steroids to win competitions is wilding by cheating against his rivals and deceiving his fans.

Whereas all wilding behavior hurts others, not all hurtful behavior is wilding. If I get angry at a friend, I may hurt him, but that does not necessarily make it wilding. Such anger may be justified because it was motivated by a wrong done to me, and it may ultimately serve to repair the relationship even if I am mistaken. Interpersonal relations inevitably involve misunderstanding, aggression, and hurt, which degrade into expressive wilding only when the hurt is intentional and purely self-indulgent, and when the perpetrator is indifferent to the pain inflicted on the other. Motivation, empathy, and level of harm inflicted are key criteria in deciding whether wilding has occurred. Deliberate physical or emotional abuse is clearly wilding, whereas impulsive acts that cause less harm and lead to remorse and remediation are more ambiguous cases and may not constitute wilding at all.

Similarly complex considerations apply to "institutional wilding" enacted by corporations or governments. Instrumental wilding takes place whenever institutions pursue goals and strategies that inflict serious harm on individuals, communities, or entire societies. Some of the most important forms of economic wilding, both legal and criminal, involve routine profiteering by rapacious businesses exploiting employees, consumers, and communities. As discussed in Chapter 4, the line between corporate self-interest and economic wilding is blurring in today's global economy, but not all profits arise out of exploitation and many profitable businesses are not engaged in economic wilding. Socially responsible or employee-owned businesses that add to social well-being by creating jobs, raising the employees' standard of living, improving the environment, and enhancing customers' quality of life may produce high profits but are hardly wilders. Systemic connections exist between American capitalism and wilding, but not all forms of capitalism breed wilding.

Finally, not all crime, violence, or evil behavior is individualistic wilding as conceived here. The horrific ethnic cleansing in Bosnia and the genocidal warfare in Rwanda constitute wilding by almost any definition, but such wilding is rooted in fierce and pathological tribal or communal loyalties, and is hardly an expression of rampant individualism. Individualism and communitarianism can each generate its own form of wilding; I focus on the individualistic variant in this book because it is the type endemic in the United States. This should not be viewed as a preference for the communitarian form, because wilding in many of the world's societies has its roots in the excesses of community. Wilding can be avoided only by respecting the rights of individuals and the need for community, a balancing act too many societies have failed dismally to achieve.

The Two Americas: Are We All Wilders?

Although the epidemic of wilding now infects almost every major American institution, cooperative behavior survives, and in every community one finds idealists, altruists, and a majority of citizens seeking to live lives guided by moral principles. Most Americans give money to charity, and about half roll up their sleeves to do volunteer work or become social activists; these are among the many hopeful indications, discussed later in Chapter 6, that America can still purge itself of this epidemic.

For an analyst of wilding, there are two Americas: the America already seriously infected, which is the main subject of this book, and the America that has not yet succumbed and remains what I call in the last chapter a civil society. The majority of ordinary Americans, it should be stressed, are part of the second America; they retain a moral compass and emotional sensibilities that inhibit severe wilding behavior. But as the epidemic continues to spread, individual interests increasingly override common purposes, and the self, rather than family or community, increasingly grabs center stage in both Americas. Not everyone will become a wilder, but nobody will be untouched by wilding culture.[18]

Wilders who catch the fever and play by the new rules profoundly infect their own vulnerable communities, families, and workplaces. One dangerous criminal on a block can make a community wild, inducing aggression, violence, and a fortress mentality among peaceable neighbors. A particularly competitive salesperson or account executive can transform an entire office into a jungle, because those who do not follow suit and sharpen their own swords may be left sundered in the dust. The new ethos rewards the wilder and penalizes those clinging to civil behavior. One defense against wilding in modern America is to embrace it, resulting in the spread of wilding behavior among people less characterologically disposed to be wilders and still struggling against wilding as a way of life.

Many Americans misread the epidemiology of AIDS as a problem of deviant and disadvantaged groups. They are at risk of making the same miscalculation about the wilding epidemic, to which no sector of the society has any immunity. Its ravages may be most eye-catching among the poor and downtrodden, but the virus afflicts the respected and the comfortable just as much: It exists in the genteel suburbs as well as inner cities. Indeed, American wilding is, to a surprising degree, an affliction of the successful, in that the rich and powerful have written the wilding rules and it is ever more difficult to climb the ladder without internalizing them.

The progress of the wilding epidemic is shaped less by the percentage of sociopaths in the population than by the sociopathy of elites and the rules of the success game they help to define. A wilding society is one where wilding is a route to the top and where legitimate success becomes difficult to distinguish from the art of wilding within—or even outside of—the law.

The wilding epidemic is now seeping into America mainly from the top. Although the majority of business and political leaders remain honest, a large and influential minority are not only serving as egregious role models of wilding but are rewriting the rules of the American success game in their own interest. CEOs who build their corporate fortunes on the backs of downsized workers at home or sweatshop workers abroad are re-creating the rules of the nineteenth century's greed-soaked robber baron capitalism. Similarly, Presidents Reagan, Bush I, Clinton, and Bush II have all helped fuel the wilding crisis, partly by virtue of the personal corruption and scandals in their administrations, but more importantly through radical new policy directions.

Our current wilding crisis is rooted politically in the "free-market" revolution that began with President Reagan. As conservative analyst Kevin Phillips has noted, the Reagan revolution advanced the most ambitious class agenda of the rich in more than a century, creating an innovative brew of market deregulation and individualistic ideology that helped fan the flames of wilding across the land. In the 1990s, a new Republican congressional majority led by Speaker Newt Gingrich and the "new Democrats" led by President Clinton launched their own wilding initiatives and raced against each other to dismantle the social programs that symbolize our commitment to the poor, to the needy, and to each other. And in 2001, President George W. Bush, despite his rhetoric of compassionate conservatism, promised to complete the revolution of greed that Reagan began.

Wilding and the New American Dream: Individualism Today and Yesterday

Many signs point to a corruption of the American Dream in our time.[19] Most Americans do not become killers to make it up the ladder or hold on to what they have, but the traditional restraints on naked self-aggrandizement seem weaker—and the insatiability greater. Donald Trump, who by 1995 had made a big comeback and ruled vast gambling and real estate empires, is only one of the multimillionaire culture heroes who define life as "the art of the deal," also the title of Trump's best-selling autobiography. Trump feels no moral contradiction about building the most luxurious condominiums in history in a city teeming with homeless people. Trump writes triumphantly about the Trump Tower: "We positioned ourselves as the only place for a certain kind of very wealthy person to live—the hottest ticket in town. We were selling fantasy."[20]

The fantasy has mushroomed, with young dot-com entrepreneurs dreaming of becoming millionaires before turning 30. The "new economy" brought the age of "me.com" in which everyone looks for a fast fortune, whether by creating a new high-tech start-up or by scoring big in day trading. Jonathan Lebed, a 15-year-old New Jersey suburban high school kid, made more than $800,000 day trading and recommending stocks on the Internet. In 2000, the Securities and Exchange Commission accused him of violating laws regulating stock promotions and made him return $215,000. This didn't stop many of his fellow students and even many of his teachers from rushing to join him in a new Internet venture that might make them all rich.[21]

In 2001, David Callahan bemoaned the new ethos of greed: "The economy of the late 1990s offered the promise of such extraordinary wealth that it brought out the worst in people. . . . The ideal of working hard over many years to achieve wealth lost traction. The pressure to pursue wealth instead of other goals grew enormously as the media focused on those winning big in the new economy. It became easy to feel that missing the gold rush was plain stupid." A young person himself, Callahan continued "I've seen the resulting distortion of values everywhere in Generation X—my generation and in those coming after it. It's hard to stick to a goal related to something other than money. . . . Who wants to be a school teacher when you can be a millionaire."[22]

A new version of the American Dream has now emerged, more individualistic, expansive, and morally perverted than its predecessors. America has entered a new Gilded Age in which, as John Taylor writes, the celebration and "lure of wealth has overpowered conventional restraints."[23] Laurence Shames suggests that the name of the American game has become simply *more*.[24]

Today's dot-commers and high rollers in Wall Street's famous investment banks are living out this new chapter of the American Dream. Youthful commodity traders fresh out of business school engage in feeding frenzies in the exchanges, pursuing quick fortunes "as if they'd invented the habit of more, when in fact they'd only inherited it the way a fetus picks up an addiction in the womb." The craving, Shames writes, is "there in the national bloodstream."[25] A dramatic model is Nicholas Leeson, the 27-year-old broker who in 1995 bankrupted the historic Baring's Bank of London by losing his $27-billion gamble in the international derivatives market. Derivatives, a twenty-first-century variant of the 1980s junk-bond craze, are part of the global financial casino in which bankers bet on currency rates, stock prices, or pork bellies to win trillion-dollar jackpots. Many Wall Street players in the derivatives game turn to inside trading—and more serious crimes—when their risky ventures go bad. And so, proved Mark Barton, can day traders who gamble big time. In 1999, Barton barged into the Atlanta offices of the day-trading firms where he had lost $450,000 and shot nine people in cold blood.

For less privileged and especially for poor Americans, the new "gilded" Dream became a recipe for wilding based on collapsed possibilities. A dream of having more had been sustainable when the pie was growing, as it had been throughout most of American history. But when real income begins to decline for millions in the bottom half of America, an unprecedented development in the last decades of the twentieth-century, an outsized Dream becomes illusion, inconsistent with the reality of most Americans' lives. Outsized Dream, downsized lives. To weave grandiose materialist dreams in an era of restricted opportunities is the ultimate recipe for social wilding.

A new age of limits and polarization in the early twenty-first century sets the stage for an advanced wilding crisis. In an America deeply divided by class, the American Dream, and especially the new gilded Dream, cannot be a common enterprise and is transformed into multiple wilding agendas, unleashing wilding among people at every station, but in different ways. Among those at the bottom, the Dream becomes pure illusion; wilding, whether dealing drugs or grabbing handbags, mushrooms as a survival option and as a fast track out of the ghetto and into the high life. Among the insecure and slipping great American middle class, wilding becomes a growth area for those endowed with classic American initiative and ingenuity and unwilling to go down with their closing factories and downsized offices. For the professional and business classes at the top, wilding is sanctified as professional ambition and proliferates as one or another variant of dedicated and untrammeled careerism. Ensconced inside heavily fortified suburban or gentrified enclaves, these elites also pioneer new forms of social wilding in what Robert Reich calls a politics of secession, abandoning society itself as part of a panicky defense against the threat from the huge covetous majority left behind. The wilding crisis, as we see below, arises partly out of a virulent new class politics.[26]

The seeds of America's wilding plague were planted long before the current era. More than a century ago, Alexis de Tocqueville observed that conditions in America led every "member of the community to be wrapped up in himself" and worried that "personal interest will become more than ever the principal, if not the sole spring" of American behavior. Selfish and mean-spirited people can be found in every culture and every phase of history, and wilding, as I show in the next chapter, is certainly not a new phenomenon in American life. One of the world's most individualistic societies, America has long struggled to cope with high levels of violence, greed, political corruption, and other wilding outcroppings.[27]

Over the last hundred years, American history can be read as a succession of wilding periods alternating with eras of civility. The robber baron era of the 1880s and 1890s, an age of spectacular economic and political wilding, was followed by the Progressive Era of the early twentieth century, in which moral forces reasserted themselves. The individualistic license of the 1920s, another time of economic and political wilding epitomized by the Teapot Dome scandal, yielded to the New Deal era of the 1930s and 1940s, when America responded to the Great Depression with remarkable moral and community spirit. The moral idealism of a new generation of youth in the 1960s was followed by the explosion of political, economic, and social wilding in the current era.

American wilding is a timeless and enduring threat, linked to our national heritage and most basic values and institutions. Although we focus in this book on wilding today, the wilding problem riddles our history, for it is embedded in the origins of free-market capitalism and the individualistic culture that helped shape the American Dream and our own national character. What distinguishes the current epidemic is the subtle legitimation of wilding as it becomes part of the official religion in Washington; the severity of the wilding crisis in banking and commerce; the spread of wilding into universities, films and TV, popular music, and other vital cultural centers; and the subsequent penetration of wilding culture so deeply into the lives of the general population that society itself is now at risk.

Roots of Wilding: Durkheim, Marx, and the Sociological Eye

More than a century ago, the founders of sociology had their own intimations of a wilding crisis that could consume society. The great French thinker Émile Durkheim recognized that individualism was the rising culture of the modern age. While Durkheim believed that individualism could ultimately be a healthy force, he also feared that it could poison the bonds that make social life possible. Karl Marx, who gave birth to a different school of sociology, believed that the economic individualism of capitalism might erode all forms of community and reduce human relations to a new lowest common denominator: the cash nexus.

Sociology arose as an inquiry into the dangers of modern individualism, which could potentially kill society itself. The prospect of the death of society gave birth to the question symbolized by the Ik: What makes society possible and prevents it from disintegrating into a mass of sociopathic and self-interested isolates? This core question of sociology has become the vital issue of our times.

Although sociology does not provide all the answers, it offers a compelling framework for understanding and potentially solving the wilding epidemic. Durkheim never heard of wilding or the Ik, but he focused like a laser on the coming crisis of community. Durkheim saw that the great transformation of the modern age was the breakdown of traditional social solidarity and the rise of an individual less enmeshed in community. A grave danger was egoism, arising where "the individual is isolated because the bonds uniting him to other beings are slackened or broken" and the "bond which attaches him to society is itself slack." Such an individual, who finds no "meaning in genuinely collective activity," is primed for wilding, the pursuit of gain or pleasure at the expense of others with whom there is no sense of shared destiny.[28]

The other great danger is anomie, which Durkheim defined as a condition of societal normlessness breeding crime and suicide. Anomie arises when social rules are absent or confusing and individuals are insufficiently integrated into families, neighborhoods, or churches to be regulated by their moral codes. Durkheim believed that modern, individualistic societies were especially vulnerable to this kind of failure of socialization. As community declines, it leaves the individual without a moral compass, buffeted by disturbing and increasingly limitless "passions, without a curb to regulate them." Anomie fuels instrumental wilding, making the individual more vulnerable to fantasies of limitless money and power. It also feeds expressive wilding of the O. J. Simpson variety, weakening the personal and community controls that sustain civilized values.[29]

Although Durkheim captured the kind of breakdown of community that is currently helping to breed the American wilding epidemic, he lacked the economic and political analysis that would help explain why wilding is startlingly pervasive among America's ruling elites and trickles down to the population at large. As I argue in chapters to come, American wilding is a form of socially prescribed antisocial behavior, modeled by leaders and reinforced by the rules of our free-market game. As such, it reflects less the insufficient presence of society in individuals than overconformity to a society whose norms and values are socially dangerous.

Marx wrote that the market system "drowns the most heavenly ecstasies of religious fervor, of chivalrous enthusiasm, of philistine sentimentalism, in the icy water of egotistical calculation." In capitalism, as Marx conceived it, wilding is less a failure of socialization than an expression of society's central norms. To turn a profit, even the most humane capitalist employer commodifies and exploits employees, playing by the market rules of competition and profit maximization to buy and sell their labor power as cheaply as possible.[30]

The champions of Western capitalism—from Adam Smith to Milton Friedman—have agreed that self-interest is the engine of the system and individualism its official religion, but they have rejected Marx's equation of a regime built around economic self-interest with exploitation and wilding. Marx was wrong, in fact, to assume that capitalism inevitably destroyed community and social values. In some national contexts, including Confucian Japan and social-democratic Sweden, the individualizing forces of the market are cushioned by cultures and governments that limit exploitation and help sustain community.

In the United States, however, rugged individualism has merged with free-market capitalism, a fertile brew for wilding. Marx's view of institutionalized wilding—and of political and business elites as carriers of the virus—helps to correct the Durkheimian hint of wilding as deviance. Durkheim, in a major oversight, never recognized that egoism and anomie can themselves be seen as norms, culturally prescribed and accepted.[31]

This is a theoretical key to understanding wilding in America. Wilding partly reflects a weakened community less able to regulate its increasingly individualistic members. In this sense, the American wilder is the undersocialized product of a declining society that is losing its authority to instill respect for social values and obligations.

But Marx's view of institutionalized wilding suggests that wilders can simultaneously be oversocialized, imbibing too deeply the core values of competition and profit seeking in American capitalism. The idea of oversocialization, which I elaborate in the next chapter, suggests not the failure of social authority but the wholesale indoctrination of societal values that can ultimately poison both the individual and society itself. As local communities weaken, giant corporations, including the media, advertising, and communications industries, shape the appetites, morality, and behavior of Americans ever more powerfully. For the rich and powerful, the dream of unlimited wealth and glamour, combined with the Reagan revolution of corporate deregulation and corporate welfare, opens up endless fantasies and opportunities. As Durkheim himself noted, when the ceiling on ordinary expectations is removed, the conventional restraints on pursuing them will also rapidly disappear. This produces socially prescribed anomie and wilding among elites based on unlimited possibilities.

A different version of socially prescribed wilding trickles down to everyone else. For those exposed to the same inflated dream of wealth, glamour, and power, but denied the means of achieving it, illegitimate means provide the only strategy to achieve socially approved goals. Whether involving petty or serious wilding, such behavior gradually permeates the population and becomes socialized. Sociologist Robert Merton wrote that crime is the product of a disparity between goals and means. If that disparity becomes institutionalized, crime and other deviance are normalized and officially deviant behavior becomes common practice. Wilding itself becomes a societal way of life.

New economic realities, including the fact that the coming generation is the first to face the prospect of living less well than its parents, could trigger a healthy national reexamination of our values and the pursuit of a less materialistic and individualistic life. The polarization of wealth and opportunity could also prompt, before it is too late, a rethinking of our class divisions and economic system. But without such a rescripting of the American Dream and free-market system, the new circumstances create the specter of an American nightmare reminiscent of the collapse of Ik society.

A Brief Roadmap:
Where We Go from Here

In Chapter 2, we examine the lives of three individuals who kill members of their family for money. Such extreme wilding is not typical, but it gives vivid new insights into the meaning of the wilding concept. By focusing on the relation between the three individuals and the culture around them, we also begin to develop a sociological perspective on wilding.

In Chapter 3, we look at the amazing varieties of wilding in popular culture and everyday life. While few people are killers, most of us engage in "petty wilding" that can escalate into more serious forms. We look at the relation between wilding images in movies and on TV and the real-world wilding rippling across campuses, families, and communities.

In Chapter 4, we look at the underlying socioeconomic forces giving rise to our wilding crisis. This requires shifting focus from personal to institutional wilding, especially corporate wilding. We see that wilding by the elites who run huge multinational companies and by allied political leaders helps create the wilding crisis of everyday life.

In Chapter 5, we look at the serious forms of social and political wilding that threaten the very fabric of society. Much of the chapter is about the spread of devastating personal and social violence, but we also examine political wilding and state violence perpetrated by government. Again, we find that wilding starts at the top and is built into the policy direction of our current political leadership.

In Chapter 6, we look at social forces and political action that can counter the wilding epidemic. The emphasis is on civil society, social movements, and the creation of community. We examine encouraging and hopeful social trends and discuss what individuals can do to make a difference.

Notes

1. "Central Park Groping Victims Rise to 24." June 14, 2000. Retrieved 2/2001 from www.apbnws.com/newscenter/breakingnews/2000/06/14/centralpark0614_01.html; "New Rewards in Park Attacks." June 18, 2000, p. 1. Retrieved 2/2001 from http://more.abcnews.go.com/sections/us/dailynews/centralpark000617.html; Cloud, John. "The Bad Sunday in the Park." June 26, 2000, p. 1. Retrieved 2/2001 from http://www.time.com/time/magazine/article/0,9171,47702,00.html.
2. "Central Park Groping Victims."
3. Cloud, "The Bad Sunday."
4. "Move to Kill Victim Described by Defendant in Jogger Rape." 1989. *New York Times*, November 2, p. 1.
5. "Testimony Has Youths Joyous after Assault." 1989. *New York Times*, November 4, p. 1.
6. "Three Youths Jailed in Rape of Jogger." 1990. *Boston Globe*, September 12, p. 9.
7. "The Central Park Rape Sparks a War of Words." 1989. *Newsweek*, May 15, p. 40.
8. Ibid.
9. Cited in Graham, Renée. 1990. "Fur Store, Quiet Street Are Now Macabre Meccas." *Boston Globe*, January 16, p. 20.

10. Turnbull, Colin. 1987. *The Mountain People.* New York: Simon & Schuster.
11. Ibid., p. 86.
12. Ibid., p. 153.
13. Ibid., back cover.
14. Ibid., p. 132.
15. Ibid., p. 132.
16. Ibid., p. 137.
17. I am indebted to Mike Miller for suggesting the terms *"instrumental wilding"* and *"expressive" wilding.*
18. I am indebted to Mike Miller for his suggestion of "two Americas."
19. For an excellent book on the subject, see Taylor, John. 1989. *Circus of Ambition: The Culture of Wealth and Power in the Eighties.* New York: Warner Books.
20. Trump, Donald. 1987. *The Art of the Deal.* New York: Warner Books.
21. Lewis, Michael. 2001. "Jonathan Lebed's Extracurricular Activities." *New York Times Magazine,* February 25, pp. 26ff.
22. Callahan, David. 2001. "Here's to Bad Times." *New York Times,* February 5, p. A27.
23. Taylor, *Circus of Ambition,* p. 8.
24. Shames, Laurence. 1989. *The Hunger for More.* New York: Times Books.
25. Ibid., p. 27.
26. Reich, Robert B. 1991. "Secession of the Successful." *New York Times Magazine,* January 20, pp. 16–17, 42–45.
27. Tocqueville, Alexis de. [1840] 1985. *Democracy in America.* Vol. 2. New York: Knopf, pp. 123–24.
28. Cited in Lukes, Steven. 1973. *Émile Durkheim: His Life and Work.* New York: Penguin, p. 207.
29. Ibid.
30. Cited in Tucker, Robert C. 1972. *The Marx–Engels Reader.* New York: Norton, p. 337.
31. Lukes, *Émile Durkheim,* p. 218.

The Ultimate Wilders

Prisoners of the American Dream

Why should we be in such desperate haste to succeed? And in such desperate enterprises?

—Henry David Thoreau

On October 16, 2000, a North Carolina state jury formally indicted Deidre Lane for killing her husband, NFL running back Fred Lane. Prosecutors contend the motive was money. Deidre, who confessed to the murder but claimed it was in self-defense, stood to gain $5 million in life insurance from a policy on her husband's life issued in 1999.[1]

Two years earlier, in 1998, east Texas pharmacist Frederic Welborn Lunsford pleaded guilty to killing his wife of 14 years, Janice Pamela, by repeatedly poisoning her with prescription medicine. One night, he gave her a large dose of methadone to induce a comalike sleep. He then shot her in the chest and slit her wrists to make it look as if she had committed suicide. Lunsford admitted the murder after his secret lover came forward and told police that he had talked about hiring someone to kill his wife. Lunsford told his mistress that he couldn't deal with the financial consequences of an impending divorce. He had paid child support for two children from a prior divorce and desperately feared being saddled with the costs of two more. It was easier to kill his wife than lose his kids and deal with the debt.[2]

A few years earlier, Pamela Smart, an ambitious, pretty New Hampshire high school media services director, seduced an adolescent student and persuaded him to help her kill Gregory Smart, her 24-year-old husband. After the murder, her teenage lover went to jail and Smart got thousands in insurance money. But she wasn't able to enjoy it for long because the real story finally leaked out from the boy and his friends. Smart was convicted of first-degree murder and sent to jail in Bedford Hills, New York, where she is incarcerated today. Still, Smart realized one of her ambitions—

to become famous. Hollywood made a movie, *To Die For*, about her venemous crime, with Nicole Kidman playing the "black widow," as women who kill their husbands for money are now called.

All these killers are "ultimate wilders," Charles Stuart look-alikes prepared to do anything for money. Smart is most reminiscent of Stuart because she was ambitious, competitive, successful, and an "all-American" cheerleader and honors student. She aspired to be the next Barbara Walters, and many believed she'd make it. Smart, like Stuart, seemed the embodiment of the American Dream.

Sociologist C. Wright Mills argued that the sociological imagination connects personal biography to the social structure and culture of the times. In Chapter 1, I argued that our current wilding wave began around 1980, as a new American Dream and a new economy began to take form. Consider below three of the most infamous wilders who committed their crimes during this latest epidemic.

Robert Oakley Marshall: "Speed Demon on the Boulevard of Dreams"

After the prosecutor had summed up the case against their dad, and there could be no doubt in anyone's mind, not even their own, about the horrific fact that their father really had killed their mother, Roby and Chris, aged 20 and 19, were thinking the same thing. Their lives were a lie. They had always been envied, admired, privileged. They had had money and a perfect family. "How much in love with each other they'd all seemed. . . . The all-American family. The American Dream that came true."[3]

The sons now knew the truth—that their father, Rob, a spectacularly successful New Jersey life insurance salesman, had indeed arranged with professional assassins in Louisiana to come up on the night of September 7, 1984, to Atlantic City; that he had arranged the same night to drive his wife, Maria, to dinner at Harrah's in his Cadillac Eldorado. After dinner and wine and some late gambling in the casino, Rob had driven his sleepy wife back toward Toms River, had pulled off the parkway at the Oyster Creek picnic area to check out what he told Maria seemed to be a problem in the tire. Going out to check the tire, he had waited for the paid executioners to steal up to the car, shoot Maria point-blank in the back, and swat Rob on the head to draw a little blood and make it look like a genuine robbery. (The Louisiana men had wanted to inflict a gunshot wound, but Rob had gone white and almost fainted—saying, "I'm not the one getting shot"—and insisted on only being hit on the head.) Rob had returned home looking strangely buoyant after his trauma, striking one detective as more like a man ready to go out sailing on his yacht than someone who had just lost his wife. Rob Marshall had reason to feel a large burden had been lifted from his shoulders: He now stood to recover approximately $1.5 million from the insurance policy he had taken out on Maria, more than enough to clear $200,000 in gambling debts he owed in Atlantic City and to set himself up handsomely for his next steps on the ladder of the American Dream. He could pay off the mortgage, buy a new car for himself and each of his three boys, and indulge in a whirlwind romance with his sexy mistress.

Rob Marshall had good cause to feel that the police would not come after him. Talking to Gene, his brother-in-law and a lawyer, who pointed out that it did not look especially good that he was deep in debt and stood to get such a huge insurance payment, Rob responded that the police could not possibly suspect him. "I'm much too high up the civic ladder. My reputation in the community, in fact, places me beyond reproach."[4]

He was right about one thing: The police themselves called Rob a "pillar" of the community. Back in the early 1970s, Rob had quickly proved himself a sensational salesman, selling more than $2 million in life insurance in his first year; in his second he was again among the top 50 Provident Mutual Life salesmen in the country. Rob and his family had moved into a big house, and Rob drove around town in a flashy red Cadillac. Rob had also scored big in his private life, capturing Maria, a Philadelphia Main Line doctor's daughter who was exquisitely beautiful and always kept herself and her sons impeccably groomed. Maria was Rob's proudest possession. He loved her beauty. When he was arranging to have her killed, Rob told the executioners they must not mar Maria's looks; he could not stand that idea.[5]

Rob and Maria, Joe McGinniss writes, were like royalty in Toms River. One neighbor said they "seemed to have the ideal family and lifestyle. You know, like you'd see on TV."[6] Everyone admired how they looked; they also admired Rob's business success and the fact that the Marshalls "were always buying something new." They moved to a bigger house, joined the country club. Maria was invited to join Laurel Twigs, a prestigious charitable organization, and Rob became a mover and shaker in the Rotary Club, the United Way, and the country club.[7]

There was not much doubt about how Rob had gotten so far so fast. The man was *driven*, the most aggressive salesman Toms River had ever seen. Kevin Kelly, the prosecutor who had once bought insurance from

Rob, said Rob pushed through the deal while half his hamburger was still on his plate and the engine still hot in the parking lot. "The guy could fit in three or four lunches a day, the way he hustled." His drive—and his ego—seemed as big as Donald Trump's, who happened to own the Atlantic City casinos where Rob gambled and where he staged Maria's last supper.[8]

Over the course of his nationally publicized trial, later celebrated in the TV miniseries *Blind Faith*, Rob's shameless behavior confirmed the nefarious picture of a sociopathic, greed-soaked personality painted by the prosecutor. In the first few weeks after the murder, Rob could barely conceal his excitement about his new freedom, not only making quick moves to get his hands on the money but also charming at least three different women into his wife's bed before he had figured out how to dispose of her remains. He staged a phony suicide attempt, giving himself the opportunity to leave "suicide tapes" by which he could publicly display his love of his kids and Maria. The fact is, as prosecutor Kevin Kelly showed, nobody close to Rob ever heard him weep or saw him show any real grief or sense of loss over Maria. In fact, Rob had indifferently left her ashes in a brown cardboard box in a drawer in the funeral home, while at the same time he put back on and prominently wore at the trial the gold wedding ring Maria had given him. Rob would embarrass his sons by his public demonstrations of his love for them, wearing signs for the cameras saying "I love you" even as he was desperately urging them to perjure themselves and risk jail to save his neck.

Prosecutor Kevin Kelly summed up Rob's personality: He's "self-centered, he's greedy, he's desperate, he's materialistic, and he's a liar. . . . [H]e will use anybody, he will say anything, and he will do anything—including use his own family—to get out from under." Rob was single-mindedly out for number one; he "loves no one but himself."[9] Kelly was not greatly exaggerating, but what he knew and did not say was that many of the same epithets could be applied to many other Toms River residents. The fact is, as one native observed, Rob was in many ways not a whole lot different from his neighbors. Rob's case, one resident wrote, was compelling precisely because there was an intimate connection between "the town's collective values and the story of Rob and Maria Marshall." Indeed, the spotlight on Rob—and the community's obsession with it—stemmed from the fact that it helped to bring into sharp definition what the community was really about.[10]

Toms River in the 1970s was full of people in a hurry, many of them like the Marshalls, recent immigrants to the town scurrying to cash in on one of the biggest booms on the New Jersey shore. Ocean County was the second-fastest-growing county in the country, causing real estate values to soar and triggering spectacular business opportunities. The mostly blue-collar and lower-middle-class migrants who flocked to Toms River caught the fantastic entrepreneurial fever. Everyone in Toms River was suddenly making deals—and then the limits on the money to be made evaporated. Since most people were new to the community, conspicuous consumption became the quickest way to get known and command respect. "I shop, therefore I am" became the Toms River credo long before it started showing up on bumper stickers around the country in the 1980s. Lots of other Toms River folks were joining the country club and driving their Cadillacs up to Atlantic City at night, joining Rob for the big bets at the high-priced blackjack tables.

Rob was a hustler, but hustling was the name of the game in Toms River—just as it already was in Atlantic City and increasingly becoming in Ronald Reagan's Washington and on Wall Street. Rob, a number of commentators observed, was remarkably tuned in to the spirit of his times. The commercials about getting yours and getting it now kept ringing in his ears. And as the 1980s progressed, Rob tuned in to bigger dreams than Toms River could offer. "See, all around Rob in the eighties," one old friend said, "everybody was scoring everything: sex, dope, big-money deals. At least, he thought so."[11] If those young kids out of business school could be making their first million on Wall Street before they were 30, Rob was missing something he deserved. As his success grew, so did his aspirations, his sense of deprivation, and his gambling debts. Like the country as a whole, Rob was going to leverage himself into a real fortune.

Yet if the resonance between Rob and the collective values of his time was electric, most people in Toms River or Atlantic City were not murdering their wives to cover their debts and advance one more step up the ladder. Rob was different, but mainly because he personified so purely and acted out so unrestrainedly the hungers driving his neighbors. Lots of others were dreaming the same big American Dream. But Rob was completely engulfed by it, his personality a machine perfectly dedicated to "making it." Rob was abnormal because the American Dream that was becoming the new standard had penetrated every fiber of his being, purging all traces of the emotional or moral sensibilities that restrained his neighbors. Rob's aggressiveness was startling even in an age of hustlers, his narcissism was more extreme than that of most of his fellow travelers in the Me generation, and in an age of moral decline, his conscience was exceptionally elastic.

Undoubtedly, Rob's "abnormality" had roots in his past—perhaps in the Depression, which ruined his family and turned his father into an alcoholic; perhaps in his chronic sense of being an outsider, having moved at least 10 times before he was 16. But if Rob had not murdered his wife, he would never have come under the psychiatric microscope, because his extreme traits were exactly those that people on the way up were supposed to exhibit—and that would propel them to the top. For 15 years, Rob's "abnormality" had helped make him the biggest success in his community.

Rob got into trouble only because his dreams finally outstripped his own formidable capacities. He probably would not have killed Maria if he had not fallen so deeply into debt, and he might not have gotten into such debt if he had not been lured by the bigger dreams and looser moral sensibilities that his friends said had gotten under his skin and now possessed him. The reckless and grandiose entrepreneurial culture of Toms River that would later sweep across America released the extremes in Rob's personality, nurturing his sense of himself as a legend in his own time, free to make his own rules and look after number one first. When he got into deep financial trouble, the culture that might have restrained him was instead unleashing his deep-seated potential for wilding.

Them and Us: Violence and the Oversocialized American Character

Public reaction to ultimate wilders like Rob Marshall, Charles Stuart, and Pamela Smart has been schizophrenic. Utter shock that anyone could indifferently wipe out a wife, husband, mother, or child like an insect for money is linked with a sliver of recognition that there is something familiar about these killers. "The first thing people want to know," Alison Bass wrote in the *Boston Globe*, is "how could anyone so carefully and coolly plan the murder of a wife, a child, anyone?"[12] But the second, usually subliminal, question is, "Could my husband do it?" or, even more subliminal, "Could I?"

Do ultimate wilders tell us something important about ourselves and our society—or are they just bizarre sideshows? Reassuring responses come from the many commentators who observe, as does psychiatrist Dr. Charles Ford, that although people such as Rob Marshall, Charles Stuart, and Pamela Smart "on the surface look very normal," they are suffering from either mental illness or deep-seated "character disorders" such as narcissism or sociopathy, that radically differentiate "them" from "us."[13] Criminologists James Alan Fox and Jack Levin describe sociopaths such as Charles Stuart as people who "blend in well and function appropriately" but are "far from normal." Criminologists explain that sociopaths "know the right thing to do" to emulate the rest of us; they are consummate actors: "Sociopaths lie, manipulate, and deceive. They are good at it. Like actors they play a role on the stage of life."[14]

When they murder, ultimate wilders clearly act differently, but the clinical accounts of their character disorders do not provide a persuasive argument for the difference between "them" and "us." The bible of psychiatry, the *Diagnostic and Statistical Manual of the American Psychiatric Association,* defines narcissistic personality disorder as "[t]he tendency to exploit others to achieve one's own ends, to exaggerate achievements and talents, to feel entitled to and to crave constant attention and adulation."[15] Criminologists Fox and Levin define sociopaths as "self-centered, manipulative, possessive, envious, reckless, and unreliable. They demand special treatment and inordinate attention, often exaggerating their own importance. . . . On their way to the top, sociopaths ruthlessly step over their competitors without shame or guilt." These are common human frailties, and Fox and Levin acknowledge that they are widespread among Americans who live in a culture that often idolizes characters such as J. R. Ewing of *Dallas,* the personification of virtually all sociopathic traits. In trying to predict when the difference between "them" and "us" emerges, Fox and Levin end up in another conundrum, for they acknowledge that most sociopaths rarely reach the point "at which they feel it necessary to kill. Most of them live ordinary lives." Distinguishing "them" from "us" then seems a bit like the dilemma American soldiers faced in Vietnam—trying to distinguish the guerrillas from the rest of the population.[16]

It is time for sociologists to reclaim the idea of sociopathy, a concept as useful for understanding a sick society as a sick psyche. A sociopathic society is one, like the Ik, marked by a collapse of moral order resulting from the breakdown of community and the failure of institutions responsible for inspiring moral vision and creating and enforcing robust moral codes. In such a society, the national character-type tends toward sociopathy, and idealized behavior, although veiled in a rhetoric of morality, becomes blurred with antisocial egoism. The founders of modern sociology, especially Émile Durkheim, as noted in Chapter 1, worried that modernity threatened to turn the most developed industrial cultures into sociopathic caldrons of raw egoism and anomie, and conceived of the sociological enterprise as an effort to understand how societies could find their moral compass and preserve themselves in the face of the sociopathic threat.

In sociopathic societies, the clinical effort to dissect the sociopathic personality cannot be separated from an analysis of national character and ideology. Rob Marshall, Charles Stuart, and Pamela Smart may be deranged, but their derangement mirrors a national disorder. As the United States enters the twenty-first century, the official religion of the free market increasingly sanctifies sociopathy in the guise of individual initiative, entrepreneurship, and "making it." As the American Dream becomes a recipe for wilding, clinicians and criminologists need to deepen their sociological understanding or they will continue to misread Marshall, Stuart, and Smart as a failure of socialization rather than a pathology of oversocialization. Marshall internalized too deeply the central American values of competitiveness and material success, discarding any other values that might interfere with personal ambitions. Marshall, Stuart, Smart, and other ultimate wilders are most interesting as prisoners of the same American Dream that compels the rest of us but does not consume us with quite the same intensity.

Lyle and Erik Menendez: A Family of Competitors

On the evening of August 20, 1989, as José Menendez was watching television in the spacious den of his $4-million Beverly Hills estate, he had reason to feel pretty good about his life. José was a perfectionist who, according to his older son, Lyle, felt he could never "do something well enough." But even José, with his high standards and consuming ambition, might have admitted that an impoverished immigrant who by age 45 had risen to become a millionaire in Hollywood's inner sanctum had not done too badly. He could count Hollywood celebrities Barry Manilow, Kenny Rogers, and Sylvester Stallone as his friends. Founder and president of Live Entertainment, Inc., a successful national videocassette distributor, his was a Horatio Alger story come true. Journalist Pete Hamil wrote in *Esquire* magazine that José was a "glittering" testimony to the American Dream of the Reagan years.[17]

As he sat with his wife, Kitty, that evening eating fresh berries and cream, José would certainly have gotten deep satisfaction from the comments of his fellow executive Ralph King, who eulogized José in the *Wall Street Journal* after his death as "by far the brightest, toughest businessman I have ever worked with," or of former Hertz chairman Robert Stone, who said he "had never known anyone who worked harder, worked toward more goals." José, according to Stone, probably "would have become president of the company" had he stayed at Hertz. Coming to the United States from Cuba at age 15, José had dedicated every ounce of his being to getting ahead, vowing to "develop strip malls" if that was what it took to "succeed by age thirty." He could not have been better psychologically equipped. He was an intensely aggressive and competitive man brimming with entrepreneurial energy. Straight out of accounting school, he had hustled from Coopers and Lybrand to a Chicago shipping firm to Hertz, and then to RCA, successfully signing on performer José Feliciano. After being passed over for executive vice president at RCA, Menendez achieved a brilliant coup by creating Live Entertainment, Inc., as the video arm of Carolco Pictures, on whose board he sat and which had gone big-time with its smash hit, *Rambo II*.[18]

Turning to his two handsome sons as they burst into the room, José could savor a different kind of pride. José had a burning desire to see his sons succeed as he had, and he had dedicated himself to that end with the same relentless passion with which he had pursued his business goals, drilling Lyle and Erik for hours on the tennis courts and constantly exhorting them to outperform their peers on and off the court. "There is a lot of pressure," Erik said, "to be great." Lyle, aged 22, was to graduate soon from Princeton, and José's younger son, Erik, aged 19, who had gotten into UCLA, was talking about wanting to realize his father's own ambition of becoming the first Cuban-American U.S. senator.

José was probably more puzzled than frightened when he saw that Lyle and Erik were both carrying shotguns. But he had no time to ask questions. Within seconds of barging into the den, as police reconstruct the scene, the two sons had fired eight shots point-blank at their father and five at their mother. Just to make sure, they thrust the barrel of one gun into their father's mouth and blew off the back of his head. Police would later say that the scene was so gruesome that it could not possibly have been a Mafia hit, as some had first speculated, because the Mob kills "clean." Erik later told reporters that his parents' ravaged, blood-spattered, lifeless bodies "looked like wax."[19]

Lyle and Erik claimed that they had gone out that evening to see the James Bond film *License to Kill* but ended up seeing *Batman*. They came back late at night, they said, horrified to find the carnage at home. Neighbors reported that they heard the sons screaming and sobbing, presumably after discovering the bodies. But police suspected Lyle and Erik from the very beginning—and not only because, as District Attorney Ira Reiner put it, a $14-million estate provided "an ample motive." The boys were not able to produce ticket stubs for *Batman*, and police had found a shotgun shell casing in one of Lyle's jackets. Then investigators discovered that two years earlier in high school Erik had co-written a play about a wealthy teenager who murders his parents for money, a creation that made his mother, who helped type the manuscript, proud of her son's gifts. But it was about six months later that police found the smoking pistol they were seeking when they confiscated tapes of psychotherapy sessions with both boys that apparently offered direct evidence of their involvement in the crime.

The Menendez brothers eventually confessed to the killings, acknowledging that they had followed through on a calculated plan to shoot their parents. But Lyle and Erik presented themselves in court not as brutal murderers but as innocent victims. They said they killed in self-defense, and because of years of emotional and sexual abuse. Erik claimed that his father had been sexually abusing him since he was 5 years old, forcing him repeatedly to have oral and anal sex.

The prosecution, however, as well as many followers of the trial, were skeptical about this "abuse excuse," noting accurately that it was one of the more fashionable and disturbing trends in legal defenses. It had cropped up in such infamous trials as the Bobbitt case, in which a sexually abused wife defended cutting off her husband's penis because he beat her. There were reasons to doubt the truth of the Menendez brothers' sexual abuse claims, among them the fact that in their time in psychotherapy the boys had never mentioned sexual abuse to their therapist, Dr. L. Jerome Oziel, who was the one to initially get (and tape) the boys' murder confession. Erik and Lyle had given Dr. Oziel written permission when they entered therapy to share their confidences with their parents, an unlikely act for young men who would presumably be using the therapy to discuss their parents' alleged mental, physical, and sexual abuse. In addition, the abuse defense was introduced late in the game, many months after the killings and shortly before the trial opened. Family members and others who had known the family well and were familiar with José's many mistresses and affairs, were reported to be incredulous, partly because none of them had ever heard any whisper of this other side of the macho José's sexual life.

Even if José had sexually abused his sons, such abuse would neither justify the killings nor constitute proof of the real motive of the shootings. There were other ways for these smart and wealthy young men to defend themselves and escape the family's oppressive yoke, including running away and assuming new identities, seeking shelter with friends, relatives, or protective social service agencies, or going off to boarding school and college, as Lyle, in fact, had done. But all of these strategies would probably have cost Lyle and Erik their inheritances and certainly would not have given them immediate access to their parents' huge estate.

The remarkable behavior of Lyle and Erik after the killings offers the most revealing clues to why they committed them. Neither boy wasted any time. Lyle dropped out of Princeton and, after flirting with the idea of a professional tennis career (he had once ranked 36th in the U.S. juniors), decided "to build a business empire from the ground up." Taking his share of an initial $400,000 insurance payment, he bought Chuck's Spring Street Café, a popular student hangout near the Princeton campus specializing in fried chicken. Lyle immediately began drafting plans to open franchises in other states as part of a nationwide chain. His entrepreneurial ambitions extended far beyond restaurants. Lyle began traveling widely to help realize his dream of making a "fortune in, among other things, show business and real estate." He founded Investment Enterprises, a financing shell for channeling the millions of dollars he would inherit into quick, high-yield returns.[20]

Erik, however, was serious about professional tennis, immediately dropping out of UCLA and hiring a professional tennis coach for $50,000 a year. He moved into the exclusive Marina City Club Towers, a glamorous ocean-side setting south of Los Angeles. Erik worked as hard at his tennis career as Lyle did at his restaurant and real estate ventures, practicing for hours on the court and taking his coach along to boost his performance in tournaments. Erik, however, did not limit himself to a future in tennis. Still proud of his earlier murder script, he believed he had a spectacular future as a screenwriter. In his spare time, he worked on his plays and poetry. He told his roommate at Marina that he was confident he would "produce an unbelievable script."[21]

It took little imagination to view the killings, as the police did, as a grand entrepreneurial scheme, an ironic testimony to the grip of a father's own deepest values on the minds of his sons. More than anything else, José had wanted Erik and Lyle to follow in his footsteps and live out the American Dream that had guided his own life. He had raised them to be aggressive competitors like himself who would seize every opportunity to get ahead and make something of themselves. "He wanted us," Erik said, "to be exactly like him." Lyle and Erik converted patricide into a carefully planned strategy for catapulting their careers into fast-forward. In a bizarre twist, they proved how fully they had imbibed their father's values and opened themselves to the entrepreneurial spirit of the decade that shaped them.[22]

Lyle and Erik were themselves fully aware of the power of their ties to the father they had killed. "We are prototypes of my father," Erik pronounced after the shootings. He added, "I'm not going to live my life for my father, but I think his dreams are what I want to achieve. I feel he's in me, pushing me." As for Lyle, he all but admitted that his whole life had been a preparation for the day when he could jump into his father's shoes. Two days after the killings, Lyle told his friend Glen Stevens, who commented on how well Lyle seemed to be holding up, "I've been waiting so long to be in this position." Later, commenting on his ambitious business plans, Lyle said, "I just entered into my father's mode."[23]

The Menendez brothers had become prisoners of the American Dream, captives of their father's extravagant ambitions. Theirs may have been "ambition gone berserk," as a *Wall Street Journal* reporter put it, but it represented less a crazy break from reality than an excessive vulnerability to the culture around them. The messages coming from their father, from Beverly Hills, from Princeton, and from Wall Street were telling them the same thing: Money is good, more money is better, and they had only themselves to blame if they did not seize every opportunity to strike it rich. The seductive power of these messages on the boys is apparent in their uncontrollable orgy of spending after getting the first cut of their inheritance. Lyle bought a new Porsche, which was not especially unusual, but his spending on clothes was extravagant, even for Princeton. Upscale clothier Stuart Lindner remembers Lyle coming into his store "dressed in an expensive black cashmere jacket and wearing a Rolex watch," which Lindner priced at about $15,000. On that occasion, Lyle bought some $600 worth of clothes, including five $90 silk shirts. "We've had bigger sales," Lindner said, "but not in four minutes."[24]

The sons worshiped the same god as their father, but they gave the family religion a new spin. They had grown up in the era of Donald Trump and Bill Gates, who made their father's career path seem slow and his fortune paltry. Lyle told Venanzia Momo, owner of a Princeton pizza parlor Lyle tried to buy, that he did not want to have to struggle like his father had to succeed. "He said he wanted to do it faster and quicker," Momo said. "He said he had a better way."[25]

The seeds of Lyle's and Erik's ultimate wilding could be seen in a trail of small wildings reflecting the casual morality of the quick-money culture that engulfed them. Even as an adolescent, Lyle frequently went on spending binges, once running up a huge hotel bill in Tucson that his father had to cover. He racked up so many traffic violations that his license was suspended twice, and several times he got into trouble with the police during his travels in Italy. At Princeton, he copied a fellow psychology student's lab report and was told he could leave voluntarily or be expelled. Meanwhile, Erik also had brushes with the law, ending up in juvenile court on a number of occasions. José, however, was always there to bail the boys out, perhaps a fatal source of support, for it may well have been that their success in getting out of small jams helped persuade them that they could also get away with killing.

The Menendez case "speaks to every parent," says television producer Steven White. "Matricide and patricide go back to Greek drama." But Lyle and Erik are poignant products of America. Their abnormality lies most of all in their uncritical receptivity to the "look after number one" message at the heart of contemporary American life. Lyle's and Erik's pathology was that they allowed themselves to be socialized so completely. They lacked the capacity to resist their father's dreams and the current era's mesmerizing obsession with money. What José had not realized was that it was not his children's ambition he had to cultivate—the larger culture would see to that—but the tender sentiments and moral sensibilities that might have prevented their ambition from metastasizing into a cancer of wilding.

Then and Now: An American Tragedy

In 1925, *An American Tragedy,* by Theodore Dreiser, was published. One of the country's great works of literature, it is about a young man, Clyde Griffiths, who plots to kill his pregnant girlfriend, Roberta, so that he can take up with a woman who is rich and well connected. The story is based on a real murder committed in 1906 by Chester Gillette, a New Yorker who drowned his pregnant girlfriend to be free to pursue a woman in high society. The striking resemblance of Dreiser's protagonist to both Lyle and Erik Menendez, and to other contemporary men in a hurry such as Charles Stuart and Rob Marshall, suggests that wilding, even ultimate wilding, is not new. But if the parallels tell us something important about the deep historical roots of American wilding, there are also noteworthy contrasts that hint at how the virus has mutated for the worse.

Like Erik and Lyle, Clyde was an authentic prisoner of the American Dream (as, presumably, was the real Chester Gillette, for, as H. L. Mencken notes, Dreiser stayed "close to the facts and came close to a literal reporting"). When Dreiser described Clyde as "bewitched" by wealth, as a personification of desire for all the glitter and beauty that money can buy, he could have been describing Erik and Lyle. Indeed, Dreiser saw young Clyde as so vulnerable to the seductive temptations that surrounded him, so helpless in the face of the material pleasures just beyond his reach, that Dreiser asked whether the real guilt for the crime lay not with Clyde but with the culture that debased him. Perhaps future novelists or historians will instructively engage the same questions about the Menendez brothers, whose vulnerability to modern capitalist seduction is one of the most poignant aspects of their identity.

Dreiser selected the Gillette case, as critic Lawrence Hussman informs us, because he considered it "typical enough to warrant treatment as particularly American." Dreiser recognized that whatever psychological pathology was involved could be understood only in the context of a diagnosis of the health of American society and an inquiry into the moral ambiguity of the American Dream. *An American Tragedy* was compelling to millions of Americans in the 1920s because it held up a mirror in which they could see their collective reflection. The novel's success suggests that there was something of Clyde in many Americans of his era, which tells us how deeply the wilding virus had already insinuated itself into American life. Indeed, as early as the robber baron era of the late 1800s, the wilding streak in American culture had become too obvious to ignore, a matter of preoccupation for satirist Mark Twain, philosopher Henry David Thoreau, and critic Lincoln Steffens.[26]

Yet if Dreiser's work suggests that wilding defines a continuity, not a break, in American life, it also hints at how things have changed. Unlike Rob Marshall or Erik and Lyle Menendez, Clyde could not actually go through with his diabolical scheme. After becoming obsessed with plans to kill his girlfriend, he lures her into a canoe with the intent of drowning her, but, whether out of weakness or moral compunction, he cannot do it. His problem is solved only because she accidentally falls into the water, along with Clyde himself. Clyde does not try to save her, partly out of fear that her thrashing about will drown him, too, but that is quite different from deliberate murder. Perhaps in the America of 1925 it was still not credible to Dreiser or his audience that anyone could actually carry out such a crime, although the real Chester Gillette was only one of a number of such accused killers in the first quarter of the twentieth century. While such murders still shock the public, Americans today, according to pollsters, not only believe that such crimes can be committed but, as noted earlier, worry whether their spouses, or they themselves, could succumb to the impulse.

That the constraints on wilding may have weakened over the last 75 years is suggested further by the centrality of the theme of guilt and moral responsibility in Dreiser's work. Clyde is a morally weak character, but he is not entirely devoid of conscience. After Roberta's death, Clyde is not able to absolve himself of responsibility because he is plagued by the question of whether he was guilty of not trying to save her. In contrast, the most extraordinary aspect of Rob Marshall and the Menendez brothers is their apparent lack of remorse. Friends of Rob Marshall, Erik and Lyle Menendez, Pamela Smart, and Charles Stuart all commented on how well they looked after the killings; indeed, they all seemed happier and better adjusted after their violent deeds and never appeared to suffer even twinges of conscience.

Dreiser's *An America Tragedy* is ultimately an indictment of the American Dream. The "primary message of the book," Lawrence Hussman reminds us, concerns the "destructive materialistic goals" that obsess Clyde and drive him to his murderous plot. Dreiser refused to accept that the evil could be explained away by Clyde's moral weakness or some presumed individual psychopathology; it was only the inability to question "some of the basic assumptions on which American society is based" that could lead anyone to that line of thinking. Dreiser himself concluded that Clyde had to be held morally accountable but that society was the ultimate perpetrator of the crime. He implicitly instructed his readers that such American tragedies would recur until the country finally triumphed over its obsessions with materialism and ego and rediscovered its moral compass.

Dreiser's musings on the American Dream remain stunningly relevant today, and the book is an eerie prophecy of current cases of wilding. But if Dreiser saw how the American Dream of his era could beget extreme individual wilding, he could not have foreseen the historical developments that have made the dream a recipe for a wilding epidemic. In Dreiser's day, the "American Century" was dawning on a glorious future; the prosperity of the 1920s was a harbinger of a new era of plenty in which all Americans could reasonably look forward to their share of an apparently endlessly expanding American pie. Despite the dark side of the materialistic preoccupation, which divided people as they competed for the biggest slices, the Dream also brought Americans together, for as long as the pie was growing, everybody could win.

It took a new age of limits and decline, during which growing numbers of Americans would see their share of the pie shrinking and others see it permanently removed from the table, to set the stage for a full-blown wilding epidemic. Dreiser saw a foreshadowing of this in the Great Depression, which turned him toward socialism. But America pulled together in the 1930s, and the wilding virus was kept largely in check, as I discuss in Chapter 6. It would take a very different set of economic and political reversals, half a century later, to fuel the kind of wilding epidemic that Dreiser vaguely anticipated but never experienced.

It is apt testimony to Dreiser, as well as to the ferocious spread of the epidemic he could only dimly envisage, to mention in conclusion the rapidly growing crowd of modern-day Chester Gillettes. In addition to the Menendez brothers, Charles Stuart is among the most remarkable Gillette "look-alikes," not only because he killed his pregnant wife but because, like Chester, he was from a working-class background and disposed of his wife because she had become an impediment to his upward mobility. Stuart, of course, trumped Gillette's achievement by collecting several hundred thousand dollars in insurance money.

38

Susan Smith: Infanticide and the Honor Student

Susan Smith, now serving life in prison, hauntingly evokes Dreiser's theme. Smith is the young mother from Union, South Carolina, who confessed to strapping her two young sons—Michael, aged 3, and Alex, aged 14 months—into their car seats in her Mazda and driving the car onto a boat ramp leading into John D. Long Lake. She watched as the vehicle rolled into the water, carrying her two trusting infants to a grave at the bottom of the lake. The car sank slowly, still floating as the infants cried plaintively for their mother, who had run off to give her alibi to police.

Because Smith initially told police that the kids had been kidnapped by a gun-toting black man, reporters have compared her to Charles Stuart, who had concocted a similar racist story to throw off Boston police. Like Stuart, Smith triggered a national firestorm of self-examination. Americans everywhere wondered how a hardworking, church-going, honor society graduate in South Carolina's "City of Hospitality" could commit such a horrifying double murder.

Pundits and politicians offered their own explanations, including former Speaker of the U.S. House of Representatives Newt Gingrich, who at the time of the killings on October 25, 1994, was one of the most powerful politicians in America. Gingrich said the Smith murders showed "the sickness of our society" and was a "reason to vote Republican." But Gingrich, once a history professor, should have noticed the eerie resemblance of Smith to Chester Gillette and realized that both Smith and Gillette had deeply imbibed the intensely individualistic version of the American Dream that Gingrich was selling.[27]

The relevance of Dreiser's novel and the American Dream to the Smith saga began with Smith's mother, Linda Sue, who in 1977 divorced her first husband, a blue-collar worker named Harry Ray Vaughan, to marry a stockbroker. Vaughan, Susan Smith's father, committed suicide a year after Linda Sue left him to "marry up."

Susan Smith's romantic ambitions resemble her mother's and are intimately tied to the murders. Shortly before the killings, Smith had separated from her own blue-collar husband and had started to date Tom Findlay, the wealthy son of a corporate raider. Tom's father owned the textile factory where Susan worked as a secretary. Smith was struggling financially, living on $125 a week of child support and a $325 weekly salary; she found it hard to meet her $344 monthly payments on her red-brick house. Susan dreamed of marrying Tom, who lived in a plush mansion called "the Castle." Tom, who was known to secretaries in the office as "the Catch," was feverishly pursued by many local women, and he complained to one friend not long before the killing, "Why can't I meet a nice single woman? Everyone at work wants to go out with me because of my money. But I don't want a woman with children—there are so many complications."[28]

Police regard the trigger event as the letter Tom sent Susan on October 18, in which he broke off their relationship, explaining that he "did not want the responsibility of children." Susan got painful evidence of Tom's seriousness about leaving and enjoying a less encumbered life when, only hours before she killed the children who had become the obstruction to her dreams, she found Tom in a bar flirting with three pretty single women.

After her confession, speculation in Union was rife that she did it for the money. In her confession, she wrote that she had "never been so low" because of her financial problems and that Findlay's rejection meant the loss not only of love but of the wealthiest man in the county. Police believed that Smith's desperation "to jump from the listing boat of the working class" appeared to be "a major motive" for her crime.[29]

There are eerie similarities with the Dreiser story, down to the detail of drowning as the way to free oneself for marrying up. Like Gillette, Susan and her mother both saw marriage as their path to the American Dream. Known in high school as the most "all-American," Susan found it too painful to see her dream slip away. Wealthy Tom Findlay was the ticket, and Susan saw no way to keep him other than killing her own children.

Susan Smith and the whole rogues' gallery of modern-day Dreiser characters are just the tip of the iceberg—not only of the larger wilding epidemic but of the roster of ultimate wilders, male and female, rich and poor, who are now grabbing headlines. Experts conservatively estimate that hundreds of such calculated, cold-blooded family murders for money have taken place in the past decade. What is striking is not just the numbers, but the percentage of those who were described by friends, associates, and the police as all-American types, defying all suspicion because they so purely embodied the qualities and the success that Americans idealize. Most Americans, of course, do not become killers, but as we see in the next chapter, an epidemic of lesser wilding has consumed much of popular culture and marks the lives of millions of ordinary Americans.

Notes

1. "Wife of Slain NFL Player Indicted for Murder." October 17, 2000. Retrieved 2/2001 from http://cnews.tribune.com/news/story/0,1162, wbdc-sports-68648,00.html.

2. "East Texas Pharmacist Pleads Guilty to Wife's Murder." March 11, 1998. Retrieved 2/2001 from http://www.reporternews.com/texas/murd0311.html.

3. McGinniss, Joe. 1989. *Blind Faith*. New York: Signet, p. 420.

4. Ibid., p. 62.

5. Ibid., p. 86.

6. Ibid., p. 89.

7. Ibid., p. 87.

8. Ibid., p. 308.

9. Ibid., p. 414.

10. Ibid., p. 297.

11. Ibid., p. 436.

12. Bass, Alison. 1990. "Cold-Blooded Killers Rarely Stand Out from the Crowd." *Boston Globe,* January 15, p. 34.

13. Ibid.

14. Fox, James Alan and Jack Levin. 1990. "Inside the Mind of Charles Stuart." *Boston Magazine,* April, pp. 66ff.

15. Bass, "Cold-Blooded Killers," p. 34.

16. Fox and Levin, "Inside the Mind of Charles Stuart."

17. Hamil, Pete. 1990. "Murder on Mulholland." *Esquire*, June, pp. 67–71.

18. Hughes, Kathleen and David Jefferson. 1990. "Why Would Brothers Who Had Everything Murder Their Parents?" *Wall Street Journal,* March 20, p. A1.

19. "A Beverly Hills Paradise Lost." *Time,* March 26, 1990, pp. 64ff.

20. Ibid. p. 69.

21. Hughes and Jefferson, "Why Would Brothers?" p. A10.

22. "A Beverly Hills Paradise," p. 69.

23. Ibid. p. 72; Hughes and Jefferson, "Why Would Brothers?" p. 1.

24. "A Beverly Hills Paradise," p. 69.

25. Hughes and Jefferson "Why Would Brothers?" p. 1.

26. Hussman, Lawrence. 1983. *Dreiser and His Fiction*. Philadelphia: University of Pennsylvania Press.

27. Sennott, Charles M. 1994. "Kin Have Misgivings about Death Penalty." *Boston Globe,* November 8, p. 10.

28. Adler, Jerry. 1994. "Innocents Lost," *Newsweek,* November 14, pp. 27ff. See also "Night That Turned Mom into a Killer." 1994. *National Enquirer,* November 14, pp. 28ff.

29. Sennott, Charles M. 1994. "Bid to Climb Social Ladder Seen in Smith's Fall to Despair." *Boston Globe,* November 8, pp. 1, 10.

3

Cheaters, Cynics, Dot-Commers, and Survivors

Wilding Culture in the Media and Everyday Life

This whole world is wild at heart and weird on top.
—"Lula" in *Wild at Heart,* 1990

In September 2000, five teenagers in Queens, New York, were arrested for ordering take-out food from a Chinese restaurant and allegedly bludgeoning the owner to death when he personally delivered the order. They had no grudge against the owner; they just killed, police said, for a free meal of shrimp egg foo yung and chicken with broccoli. A few months later in Reading, Massachusetts, near Boston, one hockey dad assaulted and killed another dad, the latest in a string of attacks across the country by fathers against coaches or players or other parents. On December 4, 2000, Shirley Henson, 41, from a Birmingham, Alabama, suburb, was sentenced to a 13-year jail sentence after shooting to death another driver, Gina Foster, a 34-year-old mother of three, in an infamous incidence of road rage.[1]

But it is perhaps not such extreme acts of wilding but the small wildings that ripple through our daily experiences that are most revealing. *Boston Globe* columnist Susan Trausch satirizes her own propensity for wilding: "An extra ten bucks dropped out of the automatic teller machine the other day and I didn't give it back." There were, after all, Trausch explains, "no guards. No middleman. . . . The machine doesn't ask questions." Trausch "grabbed the bills" and stifled "the impulse to shout, 'I won!'" Later, she asks herself, "Is this why the world is a mess? People don't want to be chumps so they say, 'I'll get mine now,' and then they grab an illicit brownie from the pastry tray of life. And oh, the noise we make if we don't get what we consider ours! If, for instance, only forty dollars had come out of the slot instead of fifty dollars, my outrage would have echoed in the aisles from aerosols to zucchini." But beating the system "made me want to play again," Trausch admits. "Maybe there was a gear loose. Maybe hundreds of dollars would come out." Trausch concludes that although she'd "like to report that at least the illicit money went to charity, it didn't. I blew it on lottery tickets."[2]

Trausch's lingering moral pangs are quite unusual. One sociologist laughed after reading her story, speculating that he and most other Americans would have pocketed the illicit greenback without a second thought, with no flickering of the conscience whatsoever. According to Queens, New York, school board member Jimmy Sullivan, a streetwise, savvy observer of American life, "Everybody cheats." It "isn't just some people," Sullivan emphasizes pointedly, "It's 95 percent of the people. Some cheat a little. Some cheat a lot. You work in an office, you take home supplies. People work at a construction site, they take home two-by-fours. Unfortunately, we've become a nation of petty crooks." Admitting to a reporter that his main concern as a school board official was patronage jobs for his "people"—white political cronies in his clubhouse—Sullivan makes no apologies. Everybody is doing it, cheating to get theirs, especially now that times are getting tougher. Sullivan certainly knows what he's talking about, at least regarding the New York City school system, where three-quarters of the city's school boards have been under investigation and half are believed to be corrupt. Sullivan himself was manipulating a multimillion-dollar budget to build his own corrupt school fiefdom. Sullivan explains, "We're a nation of fucks and gangsters because that's what we glorify in Americana." It's all part of the American Dream today.[3]

Sullivan pled guilty to using coercion to support institutionalized cronyism. He had not counted on the fact that there are still honest people like his school superintendent, Coleman Genn, who switched from working with Sullivan to wearing a hidden microphone for an independent commission investigating school corruption. Genn is part of the "second America" discussed in Chapter 1, the majority of Americans who have been touched but not debased by the wilding epidemic and continue to struggle honorably to maintain their integrity. Sullivan, nonetheless, puts his finger on a contradiction tearing America apart in the final decade of the century. The pushers of dreams, the creators of "Americana," are feverishly selling the high-roller version of the American Dream in movies, magazines, and the ubiquitous video. While Americans are being willingly seduced, swimming in exquisitely alluring images of the pleasures only money can buy, money itself is getting harder to come by for a large percentage of the population. As Americans dream big, economic shadows are lengthening and darkening. This contradiction between the glamorous life on the screen and the contrasting opportunities of real life has the potential to spread the epidemic deeply into the "second America" that, until now, has kept it at bay.

Revving Up the Dream Machine:
Hollywood Goes Wild

Tom Cruise is a silver-screen idol, a star of stars in America's most enchanting dream factory. Cruise established himself early in the 1980s in a movie called *Risky Business*, which helped mold the fantasies of the Reagan era. Cruise played the modern suburban Huck Finn who finally makes good. A disappointment scholastically to his straight-arrow parents, whose dream is to get him into Princeton, Cruise enjoys going on joyrides in the family Porsche far more than studying for College Board exams. But one class—on business entrepreneurship—finally does wake him up. In a Reaganesque revelation, Cruise realizes that by starting his own brothel, he can make it big and have fun, too. When his parents pack off for a vacation, he launches his business in grand entrepreneurial fashion, turning his suburban family home into a whorehouse. Cruise is transformed; the young goof-off becomes a zealously ambitious entrepreneur rivaling any Wall Street trader in his detailed attention to markets, customers, and finances. In a morality play for our times, Cruise's business is a huge success. As young women and clients traipse in, Cruise stands at the door counting the dollars, his charming, impish grin stretching from ear to ear. The skeptical Princeton admissions officer who comes to visit is so impressed that he awards Cruise the admission ticket to Princeton that his parents had dreamed of.

In a later hit film, *The Firm*, Cruise graduates from law school and heads toward his first job as a tax lawyer, lured by a firm's offer of a six figure starting salary, payment of all his education debts, subsidized membership in the local country club, and a lavish home and car also financed by the firm. Born poor, Cruise is hungry for success and eager to play the game. His mentor at the firm, played by Gene Hackman, instructs him from the start that billing is the most important thing to worry about and that he should bill the time he spends driving in the car or going to the bathroom. His mentor also tells him that "being a tax lawyer has nothing to do with the law—it's a game. We teach the rich how to play it so they can stay rich." Cruise's firm itself stays rich by deeply involving itself with organized crime, socializing all its young recruits into a crooked professional world in which loyalty to the firm overrides loyalty not only to the law but to all moral scruples as well.

Cruise is part of a contemporary crop of male movie stars, such as Sylvester Stallone, Bruce Willis, Wesley Snipes, Michael Douglas, John Cusack, James Spader, and John Malkovich, whose roles differ strikingly from those of the earlier generation of stars such as Dustin Hoffman, Al Pacino, and Robert DeNiro. In movies such as *Midnight Cowboy, Serpico,* and *Mean Streets,* Hoffman, Pacino, and DeNiro portrayed alienated, tormented antiheroes, struggling with and finally rejecting the values of society. In contrast, the new breed of stars are competitive "glamour boys . . . not motivated by hostility or angst but by the desire to succeed." They do not "question themselves or society." They make a lot of money and have fun doing it, not letting moral compunctions interfere with their pleasures in winning big. In *Wall Street,* Michael Douglas's character speaks unabashedly for Wall Street financier Ivan Boesky when he proclaims that "greed is good."[4]

The current stars symbolize an economic revolution in Hollywood that transformed the dreams being pumped out to wide-eyed audiences. In the 1960s and early 1970s, Warner Brothers, United Artists, MGM, and 20th Century Fox were still independent studios. Politically sensitized directors often enjoyed great control, creating probing films about Vietnam, nuclear power, and other issues of the day. But by the 1980s, large multinationals had bought up virtually all the studios, installing new hard-nosed executives and business-minded producers who reined in the directors and helped rewrite the scripts. The great Hollywood Dream Machine, as Meryl Streep pointed out, was now securely programmed to the bottom line.[5]

Hollywood increasingly mirrors the meaner and nastier spirit of making it. In *The Player,* Tim Robbins models the hypercompetitive wilding mentality of the big-time Hollywood producer who wheels and deals to get the scripts with the biggest bottom-line payoff, while happily prostituting the artistic sensibility of his writers. Robbins also seduces the girlfriend of a writer he kills in a fit of rage, attracted to the callousness of a woman who shows no remorse about sleeping with her boyfriend's executioner.

In *The Object of Beauty,* John Malkovich and Andie MacDowell model the wilding ethos of smaller-time operators who team up to defraud an insurance company as part of their white-collar-crime career, furiously conning everyone, including each other. Con artists appear everywhere in 1990s films, including *The Grifters,* a movie about a remarkable trio of mother, son, and girlfriend who are intertwined in surprisingly complex relations of mutual rip-offs. The mother, at one point, tries to seduce her son after failing to steal his money and inadvertently kills him during an effort to rob him, a scene evocative of the Ik. Meanwhile, films like *Pulp Fiction* and *Natural Born Killers,* written by Quentin Tarantino, the leading writer and director of the 1990s, suggest that wilding for money is helping to spawn a culture of extreme expressive wilding, both on and off the silver screen, that is saturated with manipulation, cruelty, and violence for its own sake.

In 2000, *Gladiator,* noted for its literal gut-ripping violence, received 12 Oscar nominations, the most of any film that year and won the Best Picture prize. In 2001, *Hannibal*, the popular sequel to *The Silence of the Lambs*, again featured the cannibalistic Dr. Hannibal Lecter, who slices off the top part of his victim's head while the man was still alive and cuts out and eats slices of his brain. Such horrific wilding was now being enacted by some of Hollywood's most distinguished actors, such as Anthony Hopkins.

In *Falling Down*, Michael Douglas models the kind of wilding that happens when the new Dream falls apart. As a laid-off engineer in Los Angeles who has lost not only his job but also his wife, Douglas goes berserk when he gets stuck on the freeway on a hot afternoon. Abandoning his car, Douglas goes on a rampage with a semiautomatic weapon, blowing away Koreans, blacks, and rich country-club tycoons—and nearly killing his ex-wife and child as well. Famous also for his performances in *Disclosure, Basic Instinct, Fatal Attraction,* and a host of other films about domestic violence and the war of the sexes, Douglas, more than any other actor, has shown the poisonous link today between instrumental wilding in the market and expressive wilding at home.

Temptation and Survival: Reality TV and the Ik-ing of America

If the ratings are to be believed, millions of us are addicted to reality TV. *Survivor* was the biggest TV hit of recent years, and copy-cat shows like *The Mole* and *Temptation Island* were also very popular. *Survivor II: The Australian Outback*, drew 30 million viewers in its first episode in 2001 and, at this writing, is threatening to overwhelm the hit sitcom *Friends,* itself one of TV's great draws.

Richard Hatch, the now rich and famous winner of the original *Survivor,* symbolizes what reality TV is all about. Hatch never concealed his intention to win the prize—$1 million—by remaining completely detached emotionally from everyone else. While others might find it difficult to repress real feelings for other players, Hatch was the consummate strategist and schemer. Drawing on his skills as a management consultant, he seemed to effortlessly build alliances with other participants while plotting how to dispense with each of them.

The subtext of *Survivor* is that if you want to survive and make big money, you have to learn how to manipulate people even as you partner with them. The manipulation is ruthless, since it requires throwing people off the island—a kind of mirroring on TV of the culture of downsizing that prevails in U.S. business. Robert Allen, the CEO of AT&T who laid off 70,000 workers while raising his own salary by millions, said that he "felt good about himself" because he was just looking after business—and succeeding. All *Survivor* participants have to buy into a similar premise: that it is necessary to cultivate strategies for eliminating others on the team while plotting a path of success. Inflicting harm on your own teammates becomes not only essential but virtuous. Perhaps only a business culture based on big money and disposable labor could create a TV concept quite like *Survivor*.

The original *Survivor* series seemed almost benign, however, compared to *Survivor II*. Hatch "would have gotten eaten alive" by the *Survivor II* players, according to one of the show's hosts. This was intended to be a meaner *Survivor*, with what the show's creator, Mark Burnett, calls "real suffering." "The level of suffering in this season—it would make you cry," Burnett said. He was talking about physical suffering, but the commentary also suggests suffering of the soul.[6]

Other reality TV programs play off the basic formula of *Survivor* but are even meaner. *The Mole* was based on a surreptitious wilder who doesn't reveal his identity while sabotaging others. Hatch may have acted like a mole, but he was upfront about his intentions.

In *Temptation Island,* another hit show, the whole point was to test and subvert real-life relationships by enticing participants into infidelity with sexy other partners, with millions of viewers as titillated voyeurs. Tammy, a 27-year-old banker who is an addicted fan, says, "It seems so wrong to me, this whole concept of bringing these singles in to tempt the couples. But it's kind of like a car accident. I couldn't stop watching." Getting rid of people is in the mix here, too, since *Temptation Island* not only plays off the disposability of modern relationships (mates as live-in temps) but also involves repeated votes by participants to jettison others off the show.[7]

Temptation Island is also a twisted mirror image of *Who Wants to Marry a Multi-Millionaire?* Millionaire Rick Rockwell offered millions to a contestant who would actually marry him on TV. While *Temptation Island* broke relationships up through seduction and intrigue, the *Marry a Multi-Millionaire* show presented relationships as a strategy for getting rich. Darva Conger, the beautiful blonde nurse who married Rockwell on air, broke down and left him almost immediately, proving that the whole concept was somehow inhuman. But she kept the car she won, went on to pose nude, and turned herself into a celebrity.

The parallels between reality TV and the Ik are almost too obvious to mention. Among the Ik, survival is the only game in town. Relationships are pure manipulation and love is seen as absurd, an impediment to staying alive. The Ik have learned to get their greatest pleasure from duping and betraying their neighbors; every Ik is a cynical strategist, and Richard Hatch would find himself strangely at home among them.

Reality TV, in fact, creates a virtual culture that clones the wilding culture of the Ik. The only way to survive on *Survivor* is to act like an Ik, that is, find a way to cheat and ultimately dispose of everyone around you. Among the Ik, this is necessary because everyone is a competitor for the food one needs to stay alive—and therefore it's kill or be killed. On *Survivor*, the survival strategy is essentially the same because the producers wrote the rules that way. The question is why the scenario works in the richest countries in history, a matter to be addressed shortly. Suffice it to say here that *Survivor* sells because it mirrors the survival strategy that millions of Americans have embraced.

Shop Till You Drop: Advertising and the Greed Tube

As the American Dream gets bigger and glitzier, the meaning and price of survival change for most Americans. Let us look anew at how the Dream is getting corrupted and then see how most Americans are adapting from their own particular perch on the economic ladder.

Alongside Hollywood as a purveyor of the new wilding culture stands the advertising industry, the master producer of "all-consuming images." Television has become the advertising industry's ultimate weapon, allowing advertisers to mainline the Dream directly into the nervous system. Sociologist Stephen Pfohl describes a young girl "exposing herself to a television." He writes: "It strikes me that she is daydreaming with the machine. Her eyes are moving rapidly but her body remains still. She sits knees curled within her dress, biting her nails, clutching a doll. Wide eyes, it's electric." The young girl enters the room where Pfohl is talking with her mother. "Mommy, Mommy. They showed a KTL 191 with screaming rearview blinkers and a flashing rotary rocket launcher with a digital tracking unit. It was only $29.99 but for one time only it's $19.99. But you have to call right away. Can we Mommy? Can we? . . . All you have to do is call." The little girl has memorized the toll-free number she wants her mother to dial. Pfohl concluded that as consumers we have been "seduced into taking the media within ourselves; its screens and its terminals now functioning as our most intimate organs of sensation. . . . We are the media. We are the television!"[8]

The line between regular programming and advertising on TV today is fading. We now have home shopping channels, and regular networks air multiple hour-long extended ads, or "infomercials," for, among other things, cosmetics, kitchenware, clothes, and exercise equipment; these often feature celebrities, such as Jane Fonda or Cher, and seem less like commercials than cooking shows or fashion videos. On MTV, such paid infomercials for designer clothes by Donna Karan or Todd Oldham, modeled by the world's leading supermodels, are virtually indistinguishable from the regular programming of fashion television.

"Shopaholism," now the American addiction of choice, reflects the coming of age of conspicuous consumption, nurtured in part by advertisers selling the high-priced version of the American Dream. The supermodels set the tone, parading extravagant dresses and jackets priced at thousands of dollars. The super-rich can buy customized Hermes evening gowns for $20,000, along with alligator luggage for $75,000 a set, Russian sables starting at $40,000, silk sheets at $15,000, or a set of gold belts at $30,000 each. In 2001, Tiffany necklaces were selling for $150,000. Upper-middle-class shoppers go to Neiman Marcus or Saks Fifth Avenue to buy Lagerfeld dresses or Chanel jackets for $1,500 and up. The middle- to upper-middle-class college crowd settles for Polo or Ann Taylor shirts for $75, Timberland boots and shoes for $150, Northface ski jackets for $300, J. Crew sports jackets for $150, and Donna Karan jeans for $75. Although not as exorbitant as the playthings of the very rich, such designer-brand consciousness helps socialize young people into the extravagant consumer consciousness of the gilded Dream.

Downtime: A New Wilding Recipe

As the price of happiness ratchets up, the ability of the average American to pay is falling. The great contradiction of today—and a recipe exquisitely designed for wilding—may be the increasing gap between bigger American appetites and shrinking American wallets.

The 1990s were billed as one of the great economic booms in history. The new dot-com economy, with its combination of magical technology and ruthless global corporate restructuring, helped to fuel the creation of astonishing new wealth. College students, like other young Americans, came to believe that they should be rich by 30, that this was their birthright, and that they had a golden future as millionaire dot-commer entrepreneurs.

But the collapse of the dot-com economy and the high-tech Nasdaq in 2000, and the prospects of a serious economic slowdown at this writing in 2001, have put the fabled new economy in a different light. The fantasy that everyone can become rich in the information economy has soured in today's reality, and many now wonder whether they will keep their job or be able to meet their rent and pay off their credit cards. We are learning that the boom never really did reach millions of Americans, since the bulk of the new wealth created in the 1990s was pocketed mainly by the very rich. Moreover, much of the new wealth turned out to be pure illusion, paper wealth that could vanish as magically as it had appeared.

A look back into recent economic history shows that the boom was always contradictory, putting the bigger dreams of most Americans on a collision course with the reality of the American economy. In 1973, for the first time ever, the real wages of the American worker began falling. By 1998, the real wages of the average American worker and the real income of the typical U.S. household had barely risen at all. In other words, 25 years of the Reagan and Clinton "booms" had done very little in real economic terms to help the ordinary American, a sad reality compounded by a big increase in job insecurity and a decrease in pension plans, health coverage, and other employee benefits.[9]

As Americans were learning to dream big, only a tiny fraction actually could afford to live big. The richest 1 percent of Americans creamed off most of the new wealth created by the new economy. The escalation of Bill Gates's net wealth to $100 billion in 2000—more than the combined wealth of nearly 100 million less fortunate Americans—hints at what was happening. Although wealth was being created rapidly, it was being distributed more unequally than at any time since the 1920s. By 1996, the United States had become the most economically unequal country in the developed world, and the richest 1 percent owned more than 40 percent of the nation's wealth, a near record high. By 2000, U.S. median wages had declined well beyond those of most European countries, and the U.S. rate of poverty was triple that in northern Europe. Much of this decline reflected the successful attack on unions unleashed by President Reagan in 1981 and taken up enthusiastically by George W. Bush. Corporations have exploited labor weakness in the new global economy by rushing to find cheap labor overseas while breaking union contracts and cutting wages and benefits at home.[10]

While much of the boom has always been an illusion for ordinary Americans, they continue to be glued to the Dream Machine, creating the paradox that *Business Week* calls the "money illusion." They keep spending as if they are "getting the kind of real raises" that they used to get "in the 1960s." Something is profoundly out of kilter, the magazine suggests, because in a period of "crushing new constraints, the average American appears unable to lower his sights."[11]

Of course, the contradiction cuts more or less deeply depending on where the dreamer sits on the economic ladder. For those on top, whether business executives or fabled dot-commers, there is the problem, as the *New York Times* reported, of "feeling poor on $600,000 a year." The *Times* describes the misery of young Wall Street financiers and New York doctors and lawyers who feel strapped by the costs of their million-dollar co-ops. The pain is tolerable, however, as Kevin Phillips writes, because Reaganomics (and Clintonomics) unleashed an upsurge of riches to the wealthy that "has not been seen since the late nineteenth century, the era of the Vanderbilts, Morgans, and Rockefellers." As the economy declines, the rich can keep dreaming big dreams.[12]

Where the contradiction draws blood is at the bottom. The poor, no less than the rich, stay tuned in to the Dream Machine in bad times as well as good. They are always the "last hired and the first fired," so every business cycle wreaks havoc with their dreams. Their boats did not rise with the Clinton boom and they got dangerously poorer—partly due to the cutting of the safety net under Reagan and the first Bush, partly due to Clinton's willingness to follow the leadership of Speaker Newt Gingrich and his Republican colleagues in shredding it further. After Clinton's dismantling of welfare, millions of the poor were left without housing, medical care, jobs, or educational opportunity; 6 million children—one of every four kids under 6 years of age in America—were officially poor. Mired in third world conditions of poverty while video-bombarded with first world dreams, rarely has a population suffered a greater gap between socially cultivated appetites and socially available opportunities.

Blood has been drawn in the great American middle as well. As they work longer and harder to get their share of the Dream, middle-class Americans are sinking. *Business Week* says that Joe Sixpack "plunged into debt, thinking 'Buy now, before the price goes up again.' With a little luck, he figured, his next raise would keep the credit-card bills and the mortgage covered."[13]

Unable to "lower his sights," Joe kept "borrowing. He now own[ed] a house, a big, Japanese color TV and VCR, an American car, and a Korean personal computer—all bought on credit." By now, Joe had 10 credit cards, which he used to live well above his means, spending $1.03 or more for every $1.00 he earned. This credit-financed binge gave Joe the illusion of living the American Dream, and he wasn't alone: All across America consumers were piling up unprecedented credit-card debt, with the number of Americans declaring bankruptcy in 2000 about double that in 1990. The transfer of debt from government to ordinary citizens has been one of the great revolutions in the new economy.

Joe Sixpack's wife is working, which helps pay for the "children's orthodontist bills and family entertainment, but it falls short of what they'll need to send the kids to college." Judith Bateman, the wife of a Michigan Bell Telephone dispatcher, told *Business Week* that she and her husband run a big weekly "deficit, but until times get better, which she keeps hoping will happen, she says, 'We enter a lot of sweepstakes.' "[14]

Larry Williams, laid off from a well-paid factory supervisory position and now a security guard at Brigham and Women's Hospital in Boston, is less optimistic and sounds less benign: "Sometimes I get real touchy when I'm not working. I've been working since I was eighteen years old. The first week was like a vacation, but when you get into a month, you start getting real edgy, you know what I mean?"

"I'm Gonna Get Mine": The New American Cynic

It is not a long journey from Larry Williams's "edgy" feeling to anger and cynicism—and finally to wilding. Feeling that his old job is permanently gone, because manufacturing in this country is, in his view, "down the tubes," Williams is finding it harder to match his life to his dreams. His feelings are shared by millions of Americans whose dreams are threatened. Evidence is mounting that many are recruits to the culture of wilding; as in reality TV, people are increasingly prepared to do whatever it takes to make it.

Based on a national survey, Boston University professors Donald Kanter and Philip Mirvis report that the wilding mindset has spread across America. The prototypical American virtue of individual initiative is degrading into the cynical attitude of "I will do anything to get ahead and not be left behind." Self-interest, Kanter and Mirvis believe, has become such an overwhelming urge that it is pushing empathy and moral sensibility into the far background. They describe an American landscape in which close to half the population takes as its basic assumption "that most people are only out for themselves and that you are better off zapping them before they do it to you."[15]

Many Americans, Kanter and Mirvis report, believe that their fellow Americans will cheat and lie to get what they want, especially where money is concerned. Sixty percent say that they expect "people will tell a lie if they can gain by it," and 62 percent say that "people claim to have ethical standards, but few stick to them when money is at stake." About half say that "an unselfish person is taken advantage of in today's world," and slightly under half believe that people "inwardly dislike putting themselves out to help other people." As among the Ik, who take positive pleasure in hurting others, none of this strikes Americans as particularly noteworthy or surprising. Forty-three percent—and more than half of young people under 24 years of age—see selfishness and fakery at the core of human nature. Millions of Americans, Kanter and Mirvis conclude, are hard-boiled cynics who, "to put it simply, believe that lying, putting on a false face, and doing whatever it takes to make a buck" are all part of the nature of things.[16]

Kanter and Mirvis have dissected wilding types at every economic level. At the top are a depressing variety of groups eager to exploit the new opportunities the Reagan–Bush era opened up for them, including "command cynics," senior managers who consider themselves "jungle fighters" and "subscribe to the Darwinian logic that they 'made it,' so everyone else must be weak, naive, inept, or just plain dumb." They believe that "everyone has a price and can be bought." The "administrative sideliners" are another school: mid- to upper-level bureaucrats whose "view of human nature is predominantly cold" and who "have no real concern for people, save as instruments" for their own ends. Then there are "articulate players," mostly the young professionals who became the most visible symbols of greed in the 1980s. They live in the self-oriented world that Christopher Lasch describes as the "culture of narcissism" and share "a willingness to do whatever has to be done to others in order to advance." They are "porcupines whose quills are at the ready," taking pleasure in their capacity to put others down on their road to the top.[17]

At the middle and lower ends of the hierarchy are other groups, many impaled on the sharp sword of economic change and decline. Among them are the "squeezed cynics," often sons and daughters of skilled workers or lower-middle-class clericals, whose once-bright aspirations "have faded along with the decline of heavy industry. The jobs they expected have been automated, eliminated, or sent overseas." Downwardly mobile, they exhibit a "dead-ender's self-interest," and their anthem is "Where's mine?" and "What's in it for me?" Then there are the "obstinate stoics," disproportionately blue-collar, who "do not trust people . . . and seem to feel more strongly than most that expecting anyone to help you makes you a damn fool." And finally there are the "hard-bitten cynics," mainly shop-floor workers and unskilled laborers who live "on the razor's edge between independent respectability and antisocial aggression." Among their life-guiding maxims: "Never give money to anyone who needs it."[18]

Kanter and Mirvis seem unsurprised by their findings. The intensely self-centered, antisocial attitudes they uncovered reflect the success of socialization rather than its failure. Kanter argues, "The tendency to behave cynically is being reinforced to an unprecedented degree by a social environment that seems to have abandoned idealism and increasingly celebrates the virtue of being 'realistic' in an impersonal, acquisitive tough-guy world." He could be talking about the Ik when he concludes that "[i]n citizen and country alike, there seems to be a loss of faith in people and in the very concept of community."[19]

In fact, the Kanter–Mirvis survey suggests the real reason why reality TV is such a hit: It mirrors the cynical, survivalist mentality of American life today. The viewers of *Survivor* are no different from the cast. They are trying to survive and get rich whatever the cost, and they assume that everyone else is as cynical and manipulative as they are.

Young and Wild 1: Drinking, Cheating, and Other Campus Sports

The young are among the more exuberant wilders in America. Progeny of the Reagan–Bush I–Clinton–Bush II era and the most vulnerable to the slings and arrows of economic fortune, they are an ominous harbinger of America's future.

Kanter and Mirvis report that a clear majority of youth under age 24, in contrast to only 43 percent of the population as a whole, are "unvarnished cynics" who view "selfishness as fundamental to people's character." Most students do not disagree with this assessment of their generation. On the first day of one semester, I asked a class of about 40 college students, most of them economics majors, whether the average student on campus would agree or disagree with a series of highly charged statements about selfishness and self-interest. Their answers were not reassuring. Sixty-five percent said that the average student would agree that "there is nothing more important to me than my own economic well-being," and 72 percent said that the typical student would agree that "I am not responsible for my neighbor." Seventy-five percent said their generation believed that "it's everyone for himself or herself in the American economy," and 88 percent said their fellow students would agree that "in our society everyone has to look out for number one." A stunning 96 percent thought their generation believed that "competition is the most important virtue in a market society," and 65 percent expected a typical student to agree that "people do not let moral scruples get in the way of their own advancement." In discussion, they explained that most students were apprehensive about their economic prospects, fearing that they would not do as well as their parents. If they wanted to succeed, they said, they would have to focus all their energies on "buttering their own bread."[20]

On the positive side, significantly lower percentages of the students, ranging from 30 to 50 percent, said that they personally subscribed to the selfish sentiments enumerated above. This is an indication that a significant sector of the younger generation remains committed to moral principles. My impression as a teacher is that a large percentage of today's college students remain generous and decent, although increasingly confused and torn between "making it" and remaining faithful to their moral ideals. Unfortunately, many sacrifice their intellectual loves to make big money, such as the student with a profound passion for the study of history who decided to give it up and become a corporate lawyer so that he could live the high life.

Growing student cynicism has led to an explosion of wilding on campuses across the country that started about a decade ago. A report by the Carnegie Foundation for the Advancement of Teaching released in 1990 found "a breakdown of civility and other disruptive forces" that are leaving campus life "in tatters." Of special concern is an epidemic of cheating, as well as a mushrooming number of racial attacks, rapes, and other hate crimes. Words, the currency of the university, are increasingly "used not as the key to understanding, but as weapons of assault."[21]

Campuses are no longer ivy-walled sanctuaries but rather increasingly sites of theft, sexual assault, property damage, and other crimes. The epidemic of alcoholism among students—70 percent qualify as binge drinkers at some colleges—has contributed to these rising crime rates. A study of 104 campuses conducted by the Harvard School of Public Health identified 44 colleges in which a majority of the students were binge drinkers. On these campuses, nine out of ten students said that they had suffered assaults, thefts, or other forms of violent intrusion, often by drunk students.[22]

Much campus crime, however, is committed sober by cold, calculating student wilders. A Harvard University student pleaded guilty in 1995 to stealing $6,838 raised at Harvard for the Jimmy Fund, a charity to help kids with cancer. Joann Plachy, a law student at Florida State University, was charged in 1995 with hiring a professional killer to murder a secretary who accused Plachy of having stolen a copy of an exam. In 2001 Joseph M. Mesa Jr., a 20-year-old freshman at Gallaudet University, reportedly confessed to killing two other students living in his dormitory, one four months after the other. He stabbed one classmate and fatally beat the other. His motive: petty robbery involving a few hundred dollars.[23]

The view of the campus as a haven from violent crime or other societal wilding is now as obsolete as the notion of the family itself as a safe haven. Ernest L. Boyer, the Carnegie Foundation's president, said that college promotional material "masks disturbing realities of student life" that mirror the "hard-edged competitive world" of the larger society.[24] Desperate for good grades, huge numbers of students routinely plagiarize papers and cheat on exams. Studies on many campuses, including Indiana University and the University of Tennessee, show that a majority of students admit to submitting papers written by others or copying large sections of friends' papers. A majority also confess to looking at other students' answers during in-class exams. "You could check for cheating in any class and you'd certainly find a significant portion of the people cheating," one M.I.T. student said, adding casually, "it's one way of getting through M.I.T."[25]

A controversy brewing in 2000 about fraudulent college admission essays shows that the cheating begins early in academic careers. Mothers, fathers, or other relatives often ghostwrite their kids' essays, and professional entrepreneurs are making entire careers off the new trend. Michele Hernandez, who used to work for admissions at Dartmouth, opened a dotcom that caters to applicants who need somebody to craft the admission essay for them. For $1,500, she will help write and polish the essay; if you come from a rich enough family, you can pay her $4,500 to complete your entire application.[26]

Technology, especially computers, has also made life easier for the new generation of student cheaters. Students routinely ask their friends for copies of old course papers on computer disk. It doesn't take much effort to rework a paper on a computer for a new class. One student at an elite Boston university said that nobody on campus thinks twice about the morality of such high-tech cheating.

Books on how to cheat are hot sellers on campus. Michael Moore, 24, has written a primer, *Cheating 101*, which has sold briskly on campuses around the country. He describes how to stuff crib sheets filled with useful facts into one's jeans or under one's baseball cap. He offers tips about how students can communicate answers on multiple-choice tests by shifting their feet under the desk in a prearranged code. About cheating, Moore says that "everyone's doing it" and that he's making an "honest living." About his decision to make an "honest living" by writing a how-to book on cheating, Moore says, "I'm just exercising my First Amendment rights."[27]

Although a significant minority of students are idealistic and intensely concerned about others, the majority appear to be increasingly cynical about their studies and their futures. They want to "invest as little time in their studies as possible," the Carnegie report suggests, while collecting their meal ticket and moving on to the professional gravy train. Fifty-five percent of faculty members complain that "most undergraduates . . . only do enough to get by." Carnegie Foundation president Boyer, however, noted that faculty are complicit in the problem by pursuing "their own research at the expense of teaching." He might have added that some faculty and administrators are providing the worst role models, as can be seen by the growing faculty research scandal. In the 1990s, Congressman John Dingell uncovered science fraud in the biology labs of M.I.T. as well as unlawful diversion of research overhead expenditures for such things as "flowers, country-club memberships, and going away parties for departing deans" in many of the nation's most famous universities, including Harvard, Stanford, and the California Institute of Technology. Stanford University president Donald Kennedy resigned after the media reported the extensive diversion of Stanford overhead funds to pay for such extravagances as a yacht. The reputation of Nobel laureate David Baltimore, one of the country's foremost cancer researchers and president of Rockefeller University, has been tarnished by the National Institutes of Health's conclusion that a member of Baltimore's own laboratory falsified data.[28]

In 2000 and 2001, new controversies broke out about bio-tech and medical researchers making lucrative deals with pharmaceutical giants, just one sign of the growing presence of big corporations in university life. More professors are seeking equity stakes in companies or creating their own start-ups that give them a vested financial interest in how the data come out. As corporations fund bigger slices of academic research and the dot-com fever spreads among students, more professors sacrifice teaching quality and even research integrity to pursue their own fortunes. In February 2001, the dean of the Harvard Medical School ordered a broad review of the relations between the medical school and corporations funding research, including companies in which the university itself has equity. Dean Joseph Martin acknowledged that serious institutional bias may arise as universities and individual professors favor research linked to companies that can return the highest profit. Campus life breaks down as students, faculty, and administrators follow the narrow paths of their own career and financial interests.[29]

Young and Wild 2: Kids, Money, and Generations X and Y

Today's student culture transparently reflects the intensely materialistic, entrepreneurial ethos of the dot-com era. Elite institutions, where the Carnegie report finds the most acute problems, are filled with students driving expensive cars and wearing designer clothes. Students' consumer appetites—and their abilities to indulge them—are enhanced by the seductions of campus credit-card peddlers. Visa, MasterCard, Discover, American Express, and other credit-card outfits telemarket their wares to students or set up shop in student centers, offering specially designed preapproved lines of credit worth thousands of dollars to young students saturated with media images of glamour and accustomed to spending other people's money. First Financial Visa and MasterCard promise credit lines of up to $1,000 for first-year students, $1,500 for sophomores, $2,000 for juniors, and $2,500 for seniors. American Express says "get it now" and "use it for the rest of your life," promising to help students "get more out of the good times . . . fly, talk long distance. Shop. Dine out. And much, much more." Ford Citibank Card says its card can "put you on the road to a lifetime of credit . . . without a co-signer or a job." Use the Ford Credit Card and get rebates "toward a brand new car." Citibank Classic describes its special student card as "no fee, no anxiety," promising students discounts on music, clothing, airline tickets, and other goodies that won't just relieve stress but will "relieve what gives you stress in the first place."

The Dream Machine starts its work on the young early. A crisis of commercialism has consumed public schools. A report issued by the General Accounting Office (GAO) in 2000 carries color photos of seductive ads atop school buses, over computer desktops, and on soda machines. Kids are awash with ads both in and out of schools for everything from Pepsi to pizzas to PCs.

The GAO report spotlights the new fusion of education and corporate marketing. This is evident in the move toward for-profit schools and the programming of commercials directly into video and computer-based instruction. Vendors of soft drinks, cafeteria food, school computers, and other school accessories have made lucrative deals with cash-strapped schools all over the country, putting their products in the classroom to build brand loyalty at a young age. The GAO describes textbook jacket-covers featuring names and logos of companies such as Philip Morris, Ralph Lauren, Reebok, and Clairol. Clips for potato chips or sneakers are seamlessly interwoven into science or history video lessons. The new financial arrangements ensure that schools will cultivate student appetites for avid consumerism at the expense of their appetite for learning.[30]

Corporations are now engaged in a frenzied effort to reach children at very young ages. In September 2000, the Federal Trade Commission issued a report deploring the "pervasive and aggressive marketing" of violent entertainment to kids. The report found that the great majority of restricted movies, music recordings, and video games are deliberately marketed to kids as young as 12. Violent songs, movies, and electronic games are relentlessly advertised on under-17 TV programs such as *Buffy the*

Vampire Slayer and *South Park* as well as magazines such as *YM, Jump,* and *Teen*. A film industry executive acknowledged that "everyone's hands are dirty."[31]

Pamela Hage, director of Kids Link, a marketing agency in Atlanta, says some of her ads target children directly, whereas "we have other campaigns where we use the child as a conduit to get to the parents." James McNeal, a marketing professor at Texas A&M, says children are targeted because they prefer the more expensive brand-name sneakers, clothes, and toys.[32]

Increasingly, children are enlisted in advertising campaigns to reach other children. One example is Stacy Strezsak, age 8, who parades down fashion runways in child beauty pageants modeling bathing suits and custom satin gowns costing $800. Some of the pageants require the contestants to deliver commercials, as when Stacy announced herself as "the newest member of the Ty-D-Bowl family. . . . Let me into your home and I'll make your bowl shine like the sun."[33]

Growing up has lost its innocence. Unlike previous generations, today's students experience the great American pastime as an arena in which to cut their entrepreneurial baby teeth. In a baseball store in Arlington, Massachusetts, 9-year-old David Haroz and his buddies Rich Phillips, aged 10, and Marc Chalufour, aged 13, rifle through piles of baseball cards to find speculative bargains. Marc is betting on a "rookie sleeper—Jose Gonzales of Texas, worth 3 to 8 cents today—that Marc's dad thinks will move up smartly in value." David's mother, Betsy Edmunds, tells a reporter, "It's like the stock market to them. Very speculative. They know the values." It's possible to make big money with cards that hit the jackpot. A collector in Chicago recently paid $115,000 for a vintage Honus Wagner. Most kids, of course, play for smaller stakes, happy to deal in the glitzy holographic card market where they can buy an Upper Deck set for $48. Some, such as Mark Perry of Chelsea, Massachusetts, aged 25, invest for the long haul. Perry started at age 7 and stores a treasure trove of more than 12,000 cards in his closets. When this generation of youth talks about knowing the score, they are not talking about which team got more runs.[34]

The *New York Times* reported a decade ago that the materialistic preoccupations of the young were turning them into the generation "that couldn't care less." The *Times* article refers to a conversation in which a young Ohio cashier, hearing a radio news report about the missing dead and injured in a flash flood, looked up and said, "I wish they'd stop talking about it. I'm sick of hearing about it." Indifference to the pain of others, pollsters suggest, typifies the attitude of an alarming number of the young. They don't want to hear about it unless "it's knocking on my door." Young people themselves admit their self-preoccupation and indifference, talking "incessantly of stress—their preoccupation with getting jobs or grades and their concern about personal threats like AIDS or drugs."[35]

The youth of the 1990s have been dubbed "Generation X," a "slacker" population that had moved from indifference to nihilism. Suffering from dysfunctional families and an economy offering them "McJobs," they are hooked on TV, relate to *The Brady Bunch*, and have no heroes. Douglas Rushkoff says they inhabit "Wayne's World Lost in Space, both Dazed and Confused." They have "boomer envy," jealous of the wealth of the baby boomers and afraid of facing "lessness." The mindset of Generation Y, those following the X-ers, may be equally dazed, with Y-ers fearful that they might not make the fast millions that the dot-com revolution had dangled in front of them. In fact, while many hold on to the dream of fast money, middle-class members of Generations X and Y face far more job insecurity than did their parents' generation, as well as higher divorce prospects. This reversal of fortune could trigger a new wilding epidemic among Gen X-ers and Y-ers in coming decades.[36]

All-American Drug Dealing: Unattainable Goals and Illegitimate Means

"I spend long hours, night and day, in crack houses and on drug-copping corners, observing, befriending, and interviewing street dealers, addicts, and anyone else who will pause to talk to me." Those are the words of anthropologist Philippe Bourgois, who spent five years living in an East Harlem tenement, although he was not looking to score a big drug deal; he was trying to get inside the minds of crack dealers to see what makes them tick. His conclusions are remarkable, suggesting that inner-city children bear a greater resemblance to careerist college students than anyone had imagined. Wilding at the bottom springs from the same basic recipe as wilding higher up.[37]

Bourgois describes a broken social world reminiscent of the Ik. Violence is everywhere, especially among people working or living with each other. Jackie was eight months pregnant when her crack-dealing husband, a drug lord of substantial means, was caught and sentenced to jail. Before he left, she shot him in the stomach in front of his helpers. Instead of leaving her money before he was sent to prison, he had been squandering thousands on young women and "bragging about it."[38]

Jackie's violence so impressed the new drug lord that he hired her. At about the same time, Jackie started going with Julio, another dealer, who was being stalked by the lover of his ex-girlfriend, Rose, for refusing to pay for her abortion after he got her pregnant. Julio knew how to deal with violence, for he had been hired to guard a crack den where murderous stick-ups were common. On one occasion, Julio admitted "that he had been very nervous when robbers held a gun to his temple and asked for money and crack." Julio impressed his boss when he successfully hid some of the stash in a hollowed-out statue of a saint. But he did not tell his boss the whole truth. Julio "exaggerated to his boss the amount that had been stolen; he pocketed the difference himself."[39]

Julio had started out straight, working as a messenger for a magazine. There were no career possibilities for him there, and when he needed money to support a new crack habit, he realized he needed a better job fast. Like other crack dealers Bourgois got to know, Julio had become fed up with the "low wages and bad treatment" of the jobs available to him. He had bigger dreams of a career "offering superior wages and a dignified workplace," and he found it in the underground economy. After he started dealing crack, the money and new sense of "responsibility, success, and prestige" allowed him to kick his own crack habit.[40]

Bourgois concluded from his talks with Julio and other dealers that the view that

> the poor have been badly socialized and do not share mainstream values is wrong. On the contrary, ambitious, energetic inner-city youth are attracted to the underground [drug dealing] economy precisely because they believe in the rags-to-riches American Dream. Like many in the mainstream, they are frantically trying to get their piece of the pie as fast as possible.[41]

Drug dealers such as Julio, Bourgois finds, are meticulously following the "model for upward mobility" of the era, "aggressively setting themselves up as private entrepreneurs." Their dreams of wealth and success are precisely those of other youngsters tuned into the glitter of television and videos. Rather than abandoning their dreams when the hard reality of their economic position sets in, they adopt an ambitious strategy consistent with the opportunities open to them.

Bourgois hints that it is hard to distinguish these street entrepreneurs from those in business schools and on Wall Street. They are equally dedicated to "making it" and equally ruthless in their business dealings. They are prepared to take unusual risks to realize their dream of fast money. The successful ones enjoy the same lifestyle, speeding "around in well-waxed Lincoln Continentals or Mercedes-Benzes." They invite friends and acquaintances "out to dinner in expensive restaurants almost every night."

When a dealer parks his car on the street, "a bevy of attentive men and women . . . run to open the door for him."[42]

"Using the channels available," Bourgois writes, people such as Julio can be seen "as rugged individualists on an unpredictable frontier where fortune, fame, and destruction are all just around the corner." Widely presumed to be the archenemy of the American way of life, inner-city drug wilders are instead among the purest products of the American Dream.[43]

In 1995, William Adler published a book about ghetto children and drugs that conveys the same sad truth. Adler focused on the four Chambers brothers, originally from rural Arkansas, who moved to Detroit and built a gigantic cocaine business with all the trappings of a Fortune 100 corporation. The Chambers brothers were arrested and sent to jail, but not before they had created a conglomerate grossing at least $55 million—tax-free—a year.[44]

The Chambers story is not about inner-city youth as drug consumers, but as capitalists. The brothers promised their young employees, recruited from both cotton fields and the inner city, that they could get rich in a year, but only if they would give up their girlfriends and work hard. The crack company enforced strict discipline and work rules, offered health and benefit plans, performance bonuses, and quality improvement incentives. When the Chambers brothers were put in jail, other young crack entrepreneurs quickly took their place. After all, for thousands of inner-city youth, crack dealing is the only path to the American Dream.[45]

Notes

1. Barstow, David and Sarah Kershaw. 2000. "Teenagers Accused of Killing for a Free Meal." *New York Times,* September 7, p. 1; Reeves, Jay. "Woman Given 13-Year Prison Term in 'Road Rage' Slaying." *Boston Globe,* December 5, p. A6.
2. Trausch, Susan. 1990. "The Generous Greed Machine." *Boston Globe,* March 4, p. 14.
3. Polner, Rob. "A Real Education in the New York City School System." *In These Times,* April 11–17, p. 12.
4. Taylor, John. 1989. *Circus of Ambition.* New York: Warner Books, p. 164.
5. Ibid., pp. 138ff.
6. Kaplan, Don. 2001. "Host: Rich Wouldn't Survive New Cast." *New York Post,* January 11. Retrieved 2/2001 from www.foxnews.com/entertainment/011101/survivor_hatch.sml.

7. Sepinwall, Alan. 2001. "Extreme TV: The (Rear) End of Civilization as We Know It." *Newhouse News Service*, February 2. Retrieved 2/2001 from http://www0.mercurycenter.com/tv/center/extremetv.htm.

8. Pfohl, Stephen. 1990. "Welcome to the Parasite Cafe: Postmodernity as a Social Problem." Department of Sociology, Boston College, Boston, MA. Mimeo, pp. 11, 27.

9. Collins, Chuck and Felice Yeskel. 2000. *Economic Apartheid in America*. New York: New Press.

10. Derber, Charles. 2000. *Corporation Nation*. New York: St. Martin's Press.

11. "Warning: The Standard of Living Is Slipping." 1987. *Business Week*, April 20, p. 48.

12. Phillips, Kevin. 1990. *Politics of the Rich and Poor*. New York: Random House, p. 10.

13. "Warning," pp. 46, 52; "The Face of the Recession." 1990. *Boston Globe*, August 14, pp. 24–25.

14. "Warning," pp. 46, 52.

15. Kanter, Donald and Philip Mirvis. 1989. *The Cynical Americans*. San Francisco: Jossey-Bass, p. 34.

16. Ibid., pp. 9, 10, 291.

17. Ibid., pp. 27–34.

18. Ibid., pp. 35–40.

19. Cited in Radin, Charles A. 1990. "At Core, Say Analysts, U.S. Suffers Crisis of Confidence." *Boston Globe*, July 2, pp. 1, 5.

20. Kanter and Mirvis, *The Cynical Americans*, pp. 10, 291.

21. Fiske, Edward B. 1990. "Fabric of Campus Life Is in Tatters, a Study Says." *New York Times*, April 30, p. A15.

22. Knox, Richard A. 1994. "Binge Drinking Linked to Campus Difficulties." *Boston Globe*, December 7, pp. 1, 15.

23. Walsh, Pamela. 1995. "Second Harvard Student Pleads Guilty to Stealing." *Boston Globe*, February 24, p. 8; "Florida Law Student Held in a Murder Plot." 1995. *New York Times*, February 24, p. A16; Johnston, David. 2001. "Second Killing in a Year," *New York Times*, February 5, p. A11.

24. Fiske, "Fabric of Campus Life," p. A15.

25. Butterfield, Fox. 1991. "Scandal over Cheating at M.I.T. Stirs Debate on Limits of Teamwork." *New York Times*, May 22, p. 12.

26. "College Admission Offices Targeting Fraudulent Essays." 2000. *Boston Globe*, November 27, pp. 1, B4.

27. Flint, Anthony. 1992. "Student Markets Primer on the Art of Cheating." *Boston Globe*, February 3, pp. 1, 13.

28. Celis, William, III. 1991. "Blame to Share in Overcharging of U.S. for Research." *New York Times*, May 12, p. 1.

29. Kowalczyk, Liz. 2001. "New Steps Urged on University Research Bias." *Boston Globe*, February 20, pp. A1, D6.
30. "Commercialism in Schools Is Examined in a New Report." 2000. *New York Times*, September 14, pp. C1, C25.
31. Rosenbaum, David E. 2000. "Violence in Media Is Aimed at Young, F.T.C. Study Says." *New York Times*, September 12, pp. 1, 20.
32. Holmes, Steven A. 1995. "Shoppers! Deciding? Just Ask Your Child." *New York Times*, January 8, p. 4.
33. Cobb, Nathan. 1994. "A Queen of the Pint-Size Pageants." *Boston Globe*, December 8, pp. 61, 66.
34. McKibbon, Gordon. 1990. "It's in the (Baseball) Cards." *Boston Globe*, April 11, pp. 1, 12.
35. Oreskes, Michael. 1990. "Profile of Today's Youth: They Couldn't Care Less." *New York Times*, June 28, p. D21.
36. Muro, Mark. 1994. "Complaints of a New Generation." *Boston Globe*, November 10, pp. 1, 12.
37. Bourgois, Philippe. 1989. "Just Another Night on Crack Street." *New York Times Magazine*, November 12, pp. 53ff.
38. Ibid., p. 62.
39. Ibid., p. 64.
40. Ibid., p. 62.
41. Ibid., p. 65.
42. Ibid., p. 94.
43. Ibid., p. 94.
44. Adler, William. 1995. *Land of Opportunity: One Family's Quest for the American Dream in the Age of Crack*. Boston: Atlantic Monthly Press.
45. Ibid. See also Frankel, Max. 1995. "Drug War, II." *New York Times Magazine*, January 29.

U.S. Business vs. Us

Global Capitalism and Corporate Wilding

*What do you mean **we**, kemo sabe?*

—Tonto to the Lone Ranger

A Fish Rots from the Head First

In January 2001, the U.S. Department of Labor reported that a clothing factory in American Samoa—a U.S. territory in the Pacific—producing for JCPenney, Sears, and Target was abusing hundreds of workers who were held as indentured servants. A Labor Department investigator said that many workers who looked like "walking skeletons," lived "36 to a room and received bare-bones meals." The National Labor Committee, a New York–based public interest group, carried out its own detailed investigation, reporting that workers were beaten; sexually harassed; threatened with deportation; starved; forced to work 12- to 18-hour days, seven days a week; and made to live in rat-infested dormitories.[1]

On February 18, 2001, a report on the television program *Sixty Minutes*, detailed some unseemly facts about the diamonds we associate with love and marriage. Brutal wars are fought in Zaire, Sierra Leone, the Congo, and other African countries to control access to the mines. *Sixty Minutes* focused on the role of giant corporations that allegedly help finance these wars, among the most brutal in recent memory (the Sierra Leone war is fought mainly by children whose fate when captured is having their hands cut off). The *Sixty Minutes* report also explained why diamonds are so expensive; it is not because they are naturally scarce but because the largest companies exercise monopoly power to restrict supply and extract huge profits.

On May 10, 1993, a toy factory in Thailand, near Bangkok, burned to the ground, killing 188 workers, mostly teenage girls. One surviving worker who jumped out of an upper-story window told investigators that she and some of the other workers had tried to escape down the stairs but had been commanded by supervisors to get back to work. Her sister also jumped, but died. The 188 deaths made this the worst industrial accident in history, exceeding the 146 garment workers killed in New York's Triangle Shirtwaist garment factory fire in 1911. But while the Triangle fire helped to inspire an era of regulatory reform, the tragedy in Thailand stands as a symbol of a new age of unregulated global wilding.

The Thai factory was owned by Kader Industrial Toy Company, a giant, global manufacturing conglomerate that contracts with Toys "R" Us, JCPenney, Fisher-Price, and other major American companies. *New York Times* columnist Bob Herbert wrote that the company had been running a sweatshop with young girls who were "semi-slave laborers." Calling it "terror in toyland," Herbert said that workers such as these girls slave for "grotesquely low wages and in disgusting and extremely dangerous conditions."[2]

We have focused thus far on wilding by individuals, but wilding by corporations and governments plays a huge role in our growing crisis. Such wilding, as discussed in Chapter 1, involves behavior by institutions that enhance their own wealth and power by harming workers, citizens, and communities. Our new wilding crisis—in the United States and increasingly the world at large—is fueled by the predatory behavior of multinational firms that seek fast profits at any price. Such corporations collude with governments and are driven both by the financial markets and unfettered greed.

This chapter's focus on corporate wilding helps make clear that wilding starts from the top. The leaders of giant corporations and their political and intellectual allies are at the heart of the wilding crisis. They create the institutional conditions and reigning ideologies that catalyze wilding at all levels of society.

A thin line has always divided the capitalist quest for profit from economic wilding. John D. Rockefeller, Andrew Carnegie, and the other robber barons of the late nineteenth century who built American capitalism were spectacular economic wilders, famous for their brutal treatment of workers and corrupt, monopolistic practices. In the famous 1893 Home-stead Steel strike, Carnegie ordered his workers shot. Since then, we have suffered repeated cycles of wilding—the Roaring Twenties, with its huge speculative binges and political scandals, for example—that have chipped away at the nation's moral fabric.

The tenuous line between business success and wilding is being even more dangerously blurred by two fundamental changes. The first is the in-stitutionalization of the radically individualistic political economy ushered in during the 1980s and championed now by President George W. Bush. The Reagan revolution enshrined a new free-market religion worshiping business and profits and demonizing labor unions and government. It has become the dominant ideology of our times and is fanning the flames of wilding from Wall Street to Main Street.

The second change is the rise of global capitalism, the most fundamental economic shift of our times. The new global system threatens to destroy the social dikes against corporate wilding that national governments, la-bor organizations, and communities have struggled to build throughout the last two centuries of the Industrial Revolution.

Capitalism vs. Community: Sociological Prophets and Global Profits

The making of a global economy is the real business of the twenty-first century. Huge multinational companies are spreading their wings for global flight, capitalizing on technological and communications revolu-tions to produce and market their wares from the Amazon to the Pacific Basin. Wall Street is eagerly financing the new global system, helping cre-ate the global financial markets that send trillions of dollars across the globe every day at lightning speed. Meanwhile, America's political lead-ers, both Republican and Democratic, are sponsoring a torrent of free-trade treaties—from the North American Free Trade Agreement (NAFTA) and the Free Trade for Africa Agreement to the proposed new Free Trade Agree-ment of the Americas. The World Trade Organization—the target of the turbulent 1999 Seattle protests—is laying the legal groundwork for a new economic world order.

Globalization is being created by a new "corpocracy"—a worldwide nexus of financial markets and corporations that now dominates the world. There are more than 45,000 corporations in the world today, but the 200 largest companies rule, with sales comprising more than 25 percent of the world's total gross domestic product (GDP). Financial institutions are especially important, with the 100 largest banks controlling $21 trillion in assets, about three-fourths of the world's wealth. The biggest companies, such as Citigroup, General Electric (GE), and General Motors (GM), are global empires with no national loyalty. They are larger and more powerful than most countries; GM's annual sales are greater than the entire GDP of Poland; Wal-Mart's are greater than the GDP of Israel or Denmark.

The rush toward a global economy is the most revolutionary development of our times. It has the potential to bring many benefits, including a more robust world economy, dynamic growth in corners of the world that have known only poverty and despair, and even the development of a new world community. But in its current form, it threatens to pit the interests of businesses against those of their host societies, creating a new predatory capitalism based on worldwide economic wilding.

Concepts developed a century ago by the founders of sociology are powerful tools for understanding this new wilding threat. As we saw in Chapter 1, the great French sociologist Émile Durkheim argued that early industrial capitalism, by destroying traditional communities and encouraging individual ambition and mobility, endangered social solidarity and the survival of society itself. The burgeoning industrial era bred a culture of egoism and anomie—egoism reflecting the loss of community and anomie, the rise of socially unregulated dreams and passions. Egoism and anomie are fertile breeding grounds for wilding, spawning self-interest, greed, and violence that can spiral out of control and subvert society.

Globalism promises to further weaken the social ties and values that civilize both individuals and business. Unencumbered by national loyalties, corporations now roam the world searching for the cheapest labor in desperately poor countries. As U.S. corporations move overseas, U.S. communities themselves become more vulnerable, with shuttered plants and industrial ghost towns becoming fixtures of the American landscape. Thrown into competition with workers in developing countries, millions of U.S. workers face an uncertain future, and many become "temps," unable to find steady, full-time employment. The multinational corporation is itself becoming, in the words of some observers, a virtual, or hollow, community, with transient "contractors" replacing permanent employees. This erosion of community intensifies both egoism and anomie, transforming growing numbers of employees into rootless, atomized "entrepreneurs," constantly seeking reemployment. At the same time, the multinationals and their top managers are increasingly liberated from governmental regulation, free to pursue unbounded appetites for global power and vast worldwide profits.

Although the twentieth century proved Karl Marx's predictions about capitalism's death to be folly, globalism eerily vindicates Marx's view of the potential for capitalist wilding. The market's function of reducing all behavior to the cash nexus and naked self-interest becomes increasingly relevant in a global economy. Employees who must act as entrepreneurs find no shelter from the market and survive only by embracing relentless self-promotion. Major American corporations, seeking bonanza profits, pursue child labor in India and prison labor in China.

Marx recognized that the great moral problem of capitalism is the incentive of business to make money by exploiting its employees. In a global economy, this problem assumes a new scale. The core of the current wilding threat arises from the intensification of appetites whetted by the new fantastic global possibilities and from the ingenious new multinational corporate strategies for realizing them.

The Musical Chairs of Global Business: The New Corporate Wilding

The key is a game of global musical chairs—a master strategy for maximizing profits by pitting national workforces against one another and exploiting the immense leverage of capital flight. Corporations able to hire cheap labor around the world can threaten to leave a community unless workers submit to lower pay or local governments agree to various incentives to keep companies from pulling up stakes. Such intimidation has also been one of business's trump cards, played 50 years ago by Massachusetts and New Hampshire textile mill owners, for example, who relocated from New England to the South after northern workers unionized. But musical chairs becomes a game plan for unparalleled wilding when the theater shifts from the nation-state to the world—and the mill owners can relocate to South Korea or Mexico.

Here, the analyses of Durkheim and Marx converge. Musical chairs in the national arena has been a regulated game, with national governments playing the role of arbiter and community protector of last resort. Such national regulation restricts the degree of egoism and anomie that can arise from the economic game and limits exploitation by prohibiting child labor, enforcing minimum wages, and protecting the environment. Within U.S. national capitalism, labor agreements and government programs created during and after the 1930s New Deal era helped to ensure that higher profits for companies translated into higher wages for their workers and more resources for their host communities. This linking of corporate and community interests lent some credibility to the corporate manifesto expressed in the 1950s by the president of General Motors: "What's good for GM is good for America."

Under global capitalism today, however, there is no effective regulatory watchdog for the world community. As an unregulated game, global musical chairs opens societies all over the world to a purely egoistic and anomic world economy. The danger is that such a game veers, as we shall see in the rest of this chapter, toward new rules that allow businesses to maximize profit by undermining the health of their host societies. As the global economy regresses back to the raw capitalism of an earlier era, the social protections built up over two centuries are jeopardized.

Global economic wilding is the fruit of active collaboration between multinational companies and national governments. Markets, whether national or global, are always shaped by those with power, and while it may seem strange that national governments would collaborate in their own demise, they have, nevertheless, during the last two decades, played a major role in subverting their own authority as they help write the rules of the new global game. This collaboration reflects incestuous entanglements among multinationals and political elites in both developed and developing countries who have struck deals that too often are subversive of their own societies. These deals have triggered a downward competitive spiral— a "race to the bottom," as some global observers have dubbed it—among economies around the world, pushing much of America toward third world wages and working conditions while intensifying the misery of already impoverished masses in poor countries.[3]

Wilding around the World: The Third World as Global Sweatshop

On the campus where I teach, a Vietnam-style revolt is mushrooming. Students are outraged about Boston College caps and sweatshirts allegedly made in sweatshops in Indonesia, Mexico, and El Salvador. As my students push the university to stop using sweatshop products, similar protests have spread like wildfire across many other campuses throughout the country.

Sweatshops have become the symbol of the economic wilding at the heart of the new global economy.

Some students may have read about the famous Gilded Age muckraker, journalist Upton Sinclair, who ventured into the terrifying meat factories of Chicago. In his classic book, *The Jungle*, published in 1906, he described a world of 16-hour workdays paying pennies per hour in slaughterhouses producing poisoned meat rotting with blood and hair. A century later, Sinclair's graphic sketch of the sweatshop economy still scorches the brain and shapes our understanding of economic wilding a century ago.

The Upton Sinclair of today's global economy is Charles Kernaghan, the New York–based muckraker most famous for his exposure of sweatshops in El Salvador making clothes for Kathie Lee Gifford's clothing line. Kathie Lee claims to have broken down in tears when she listened to Salvadoran workers who stitched the clothes bearing her label. Mostly young girls aged 14 to 24, they described 20-hour shifts from 6:50 A.M. to 3:00 A.M. the next morning, with one 40-minute break in the day at noon for lunch. The girls described death threats for attempted unionizing, mandatory pregnancy tests, forced overtime, and starvation wages of 60 cents an hour. Managers refused to let them get up or move from their worksites, or to permit more than two daily bathroom visits. The girls described bosses cursing and yelling at them to sew faster and exceed the madcap production norm of 100 to 150 pieces an hour. Their plants are behind barbed wire and look like prisons.

Ground zero of the global workshop is China, with its 1 billion–plus workers. In 2000, after numerous trips to Chinese factories, Kernaghan wrote: "When you see an Ann Taylor suit on sale for $198, do you ever imagine 20-year-old women in China being forced to work 96 hours a week, from 7 A.M. to midnight, seven days a week, and being paid just 14 cents an hour? When you think of Ralph Lauren or Ellen Tracy, do you imagine women in China being paid 23 cents an hour to work 15 hour shifts six days a week?" Global companies, he writes, "are actually lowering standards in China, slashing wages and benefits, extending forced overtime hours, and weakening respect for human rights while relocating their work to a growing sector of unregulated foreign-owned sweatshops in the south of China."[4]

Similar conditions of workplace wilding prevail in Central America in places such as the Chentex plant in the Las Mercedes Free-Trade Zone in Nicaragua that makes blue jeans for Kohl's, Target, JCPenney, and other leading U.S. companies, as well as uniforms for the U.S. military, their biggest client. The base pay at the Chentex plant is 19 cents an hour. When workers asked for an 8-cent wage increase, Chentex fired the entire union leadership, had many organizers arrested, and built new barbed-wire fences. Conditions inside the plant are a nightmare. Managers scream and harass workers constantly to force them to work faster and longer. A 21-year-old worker, Sanchez, says, "They yelled at us, kicked us, hit us in the face or buttocks, and pulled our ears." Two members of the U.S. House of Representatives who went to see for themselves were outraged by the sweatshop conditions and the fact that U.S. taxpayers were indirectly footing the bill through the Pentagon procurements. After returning from Nicaragua, where they talked to workers, Congresswoman Sherrod Brown wrote in February 2001, "I have joined with Congresswoman Cynthia McKinney, Democrat of Georgia, a member of the Military Procurement Subcommittee, in requesting that the General Accounting Office investigate the Pentagon's role in this sweatshop. We will not sit quietly as members of the Army and Air Force support sweatshops in Nicaragua."[5]

Most developing countries have established special "export processing zones" or "free-trade zones" that offer "tax holidays" to multinationals and exempt them from environmental codes and labor laws. Sometimes walled off behind barbed-wire fences, these zones—where corporations locate their sweatshops and get state protection for every manner of economic wilding—have been described as "huge labor camp[s]," often controlled by special police forces. The most famous of these zones, and among the most important to American companies, is along the U.S.–Mexican border, the site of the *maquiladora* plants, which now reach well into the Mexican interior.[6]

Growing out of the Border Industrialization Program of 1965, the *maquiladoras* are a classic instance of collaboration between multinationals and government. The Mexican government offered corporations favorable land deals, waived custom clearance and import duties, and agreed to low taxes and, tacitly, the right to run their businesses with a free hand, exempt from environmental and labor laws. The U.S. government did its share by running political interference for U.S. companies and giving them technical assistance and tax breaks for going south of the border. The passage of NAFTA in 1993 facilitated the huge American corporate exodus south of the border, swelling the ranks of displaced Mexican workers in agriculture and other industries that cannot survive American competition. Today, there are more than 40,000 foreign factories and more than 4,000 U.S. plants in Mexico—including Fortune 500 giants such as GM, Nike, and GE.[7]

The case of the Kukdong factory in Atlixco, Mexico, which produces sweatshirts and other collegiate apparel for Nike, suggests that sweatshops remain the norm rather than the exception. In early 2001, investigations by the International Labor Rights Fund and the Worker Rights Consortium found that the Kukdong plant is a big-time wilder. Kukdong supervisors physically and verbally abuse employees. The factory refuses to pay legally mandated sick pay and maternity benefits, denies workers five hours' wages each week, forces workers to eat in a plant cafeteria where food is spoiled and worm-infested, and imposes a company union while beating and firing workers seeking to organize an independent union.[8]

Mexican labor lawyers who have independently investigated the Kukdong factory concluded that the failure to reinstate striking workers fighting for an independent union is the central issue. At Chentex, Kukdong, and other plants in free-trade zones across the world, employers are waging a war on this issue because they realize that such unions are the only tools workers now have to combat corporate wilding. Only the courage of the organizers and strikers in risking their jobs and lives has brought international attention to the issue and forced companies such as Nike to order its own independent investigation of Kukdong.

The absence of unions has meant a continued slide in Mexican wages and working conditions. In October 2000, Oscar Chavez Diaz, an Alcoa employee in Acuna, Mexico, showed a *New York Times* reporter a weekly pay stub for $60. Diaz lives with his wife in the rusting shell of a school bus and says he lacks money for food and clothing. Ruth Rosenbaum, a social economist who has recently concluded a study of the purchasing power of 11 border communities, says the misery is getting worse: "You study these wages for a while," she says, "and it makes you sick to your stomach." Another assembly-line employee at Alcoa, Isidro Esquivel Sanchez, said, "They work us like donkeys, and we come back to this" as he pointed to his one-room, dirt-floor hovel. According to the *Times* reporter, "In Acuna, as in other border settlements, Mexican workers earn such miserable wages and American companies pay such minimal taxes that its schools are a shambles, its hospital crumbling, its trash collection slapdash and sewage lines collapsed." More than 50 percent of the border workers have no indoor bathroom.[9]

Alcoa is a highly profitable company chaired until recently by Paul O'Neill, who became George W. Bush's Secretary of the Treasury in 2001. He presided over Alcoa during some of its worst abuses of worker rights in Mexico. O'Neill is now a central player in shaping U.S. trade policy with Mexico, which has emphasized, as it has all over the world, enforcement of property rights and bailouts of rich investors while dismissing labor rights and environmental standards.

Another very serious form of global economic wilding, long visible in the *maquiladoras*, is the sexual abuse of young female workers. Young women between 14 and 26 make up more than two-thirds of the workforce in most free-trade zones. Labor lawyers and social workers in the *maquiladoras* report that young women are often propositioned by their male supervisors and can lose their jobs if they don't sleep with them. Mexican social worker Teresa Almada reports that women are in "a lot of danger," both inside and outside the factory gates, and that many become pregnant and are then fired.[10]

Corporate wilding also includes massive environmental abuse. *Maquiladora* plants have dumped millions of tons of raw sewage into rivers, many flowing up into the United States. A study by the AFL-CIO found the water supply on the border to be massively polluted; indiscriminate dumping of toxic waste in unsafe, often clandestine, dump sites threatens fish and wildlife with extinction and the ecosystem as a whole.[11]

Workers are also subjected to toxic conditions inside the plants. Anthropologist Maria Fernandez-Kelly, who worked in the plants in Ciudad Juarez, reports that workers' health tends to deteriorate rapidly because of the brutal work pace, unsafe machinery, and hazardous fumes, with the most frequent complaints being "eyesight deterioration, and nervous and respiratory ailments." A survey conducted by the University of Massachusetts at Lowell found widespread musculoskeletal disorders related to the pace of work and poor workplace engineering. Many studies have found serious health problems caused by toxic chemicals and other unregulated pollution.[12]

Foreign companies are producing wealth and a booming border economy, but most of the wealth flows back into the corporations' own coffers. Gustavo Elizondo, the mayor of Juarez, says that the sad reality of his community is that it is "a place of opportunity for the international community" but has left the local government unable "to provide water, sewage and sanitation." According to the 2000 Mexican census, 75 percent of Mexicans live in poverty today, compared with 49 percent in 1981. "Every year we get poorer and poorer," the Juarez mayor concludes, "even though we create more and more wealth."[13]

The prevailing subhuman conditions in the plants and the surrounding communities are a product of coordinated repression by multinational corporations and the Mexican government, which has intervened repeatedly, using the police and the army to suppress labor protest and permitting multinational companies to evade environmental and labor laws. Wages and working conditions have declined as the multinationals have expanded, because the huge firms have worked so effectively with both the U.S. and Mexican governments and with company-sponsored unions to erode workers' rights and community social protections. These are neither free nor fair markets, but rather the predictable outcome of a global game of musical chairs gone wild.

The Downsizing of America: Globalization and Wilding at Home

By promoting NAFTA and other free-trade agreements as well as the World Trade Organization, the United States has firmly committed itself to economic globalization. Republican presidents Reagan and Bush I and II, as well as Democratic leaders such as President Clinton, have argued that globalization will enhance American living standards by increasing jobs in export-sector industries, reducing consumer prices, increasing corporate competitiveness and profits, and promoting both understanding and efficiency around the world. But although globalization is now inevitable and has the potential to enhance well-being here and abroad, the game of global musical chairs as it is structured today will prove as selective in its payoffs at home as it has been in developing nations. Its effect, showing up already in the gradual erosion of the American Dream over the last 20 years, is to push the living standards of poor and working-class Americans down and to create the kind of dangerous, polarized class structure prevalent in the third world itself.

Global musical chairs as a wilding enterprise manifests itself most nakedly in the United States among workers at the bottom, where a literal "third-worldization" of the economy is taking place as work in the United States regresses toward third world wages and working conditions, especially for jobs held by third world immigrants living here. Globalization increases the flow of workers across national boundaries, making immigration an explosive economic factor in the United States and other countries. The latest wave of immigrants to the United States, many from Latin America and Asia, are the nucleus of a growing third world economy inside our borders, based on jobs that most U.S. citizens would not tolerate.

Globalization offers employers in this country new strategies for international recruitment. Outside Chicago, for example, factories have cultivated relationships with Mexican villages that are the hometowns of their immigrant Mexican employees. These employees are willing recruiters in their villages, encouraging family and friends to join them in the factory when other workers quit and jobs open up. For companies, this direct line into remote Mexican towns is a godsend, a source of cheaper and more compliant workers than they can find among even the masses of poor Chicagoans looking for work.[14]

Sweatshops in the United States are experiencing their own revival. Thousands of sweatshops in New York City, Los Angeles, and other areas have sprung up in the last two decades. In February 2001, the *New York*

Times reported that two apparel factories in Brooklyn were accused of forcing employees to work up to 140 hours a week without paying them overtime. Two Chinese immigrants working in the plants said they came to work early in the morning and left after midnight, 7 days a week and 363 days a year. Their job involved placing finished garments on hangers, and they calculated they hung 59,476 garments each week.[15]

The Brooklyn sweatshops are allegedly controlled by a holding company with a history of sweatshop abuses. It agreed to pay hundreds of thousands of dollars in back pay to workers in a 1999 suit and a later suit in 2000. In both cases, according to one lawyer involved, "These factories are forcing workers to work extreme hours as they push production out of the door as fast as they can."[16] The dangers of U.S. sweatshops are no different from those in Thailand or Indonesia. In 1991 a horrific fire in a North Carolina poultry-processing plant burned 25 employees to death. Management generally kept the factory doors locked, preventing the workers from escaping. The plant's owner, Emmett Roe, who personally ordered the padlocking, was sentenced in 1994 to nearly 20 years in prison after pleading guilty to involuntary manslaughter.[17]

Sweatshops and the exploitation of immigrant labor are only the exposed tip of the continuing third-worldization of the U.S. economy in the wake of globalization. In the United States, as in developing nations, global musical chairs has offered corporations a way to extract from workers and communities massive givebacks and concessions, amounting to a wholesale rewriting of the social contract. At the heart of this change is the employment revolution that *Fortune* magazine calls the "end of the job," with corporations turning many workers into part-timers, temps, independent contractors, and other contingent workers. I call it "job genocide," since corporations are eliminating conventional jobs protected by U.S. labor laws and slowly creating a new workforce of independent contractors and freelancers lacking any protection.[18]

The transformation of about one-fourth of American workers, numbering about 30 million, into formally contingent workers—which *Time* calls the "tempting of America"—contributes mightily to the third-worldization of the American labor force. When a corporation reclassifies a worker as a temporary or part-time worker, or as an independent contractor, the firm immediately unburdens itself of obligations to pay for health care and unemployment insurance, pensions, and other benefits, while also relieving itself of any responsibility for providing long-term job security. Not all employees, however, will be turned into formal contingents, because globalization induces corporations to enhance loyalty and participation among a small, core workforce in order to increase competitiveness and quality. This is one of the key contradictions of globalization, which simultaneously creates incentives for making workers disposable and for making them more closely tied to the company.[19]

Since becoming a temp or part-timer means not only the loss of fringe benefits and job security but also, on average, a wage only 60 percent that of regular employees, contingency catapults many formerly middle-class workers into a nightmare of economic uncertainty and vulnerability. For example, an accountant who was "downsized" and now finds jobs through a temp agency specializing in professionals and managers, gives a graphic view of his unanticipated poverty: "I have to cheat on my taxes because I can't make ends meet. I need brakes on my car, but I'll push it as far as I can on the old brakes. My wife needs dental work . . . because her teeth are rotting. I eat one meal a day because it curbs the appetite and helps put food on the table for the kids."[20]

Beyond such economic problems, temps and part-timers suffer from a new crisis of community. Contingent work, a form of intensely anomic employment, exemplifies the weakening social ties that Durkheim predicted and feared. Here today and gone tomorrow, the contingent worker has been described by one scholar as "the workforce equivalent of a one-night stand." Inspiring neither loyalty nor commitment, such loose connections at work tend to degrade workers socially and morally. One temp expressed a common sentiment among contingent workers: "I don't give a shit about the company. I'm here to get some money, to get everything I can. If I can take pencils from them I'll take them. I shouldn't think like that but I do. Can I steal some paper, copy software?"

One temp said he felt "doubly raped, once by the company and once by the temp agency." In fact, both agencies and corporations often exploit contingent workers, sometimes criminally. The Internal Revenue Service (IRS) is now closely monitoring corporate reclassification of employees as a gigantic tax scam. When companies call their workers independent contractors, they spare themselves such employer taxes as unemployment insurance, workers' compensation, and Social Security. These savings are illegal if the reclassification is purely a paper one and so-called independent contractors continue to work exclusively for the company, as they did in one large corporation that reclassified its mail-room employees without even telling them. Believing that corporations are cheating workers and taxpayers of millions of dollars through such ruses, the IRS has made prosecution of such cases a high priority. In 2000, Microsoft was ordered to provide benefits to its growing cadre of long-term temps, who had filed suit against the company on precisely these grounds.

Temps and other contingent workers are uniquely vulnerable to other forms of corporate wilding, including sexual harassment, racial discrimination, and violations of health and safety codes and fair-labor standards.

Most have no union, employee association, or other group to protect them. One Hispanic mother, who temped for over a decade, reported being "sexually harassed and discriminated against by many bosses. They know they can get away with anything because you're a temp." She said many temp agencies also discriminate: "If you're blond and blue-eyed, the temp agency will give you the best assignment." Other temps report that they are not told their wage rate, are forced to work overtime without pay, and are required to do unsafe work. Many have to wear specially colored badges. Some are denied a desk, a seat in the cafeteria, or a key to the bathroom.

The wilding dimensions of the new system of "contingent capitalism" are intimately intertwined with globalization both at home and abroad. Nike, GM, and other huge multinational producers use foreign workers as a huge off-shore pool of independent contractors. Microsoft's outsourcing of jobs to freelancers in India and other poor nations shows that the high-tech companies are joining manufacturers in the contingent work revolution. A slash-and-burn strategy for making profits, contingent work on a global scale redistributes corporate risks onto an unprotected and remote labor force that can be dumped with one switch of the computer to absorb the uncertainties of the global market and business cycle.[21]

Domestic contingent workers similarly sponge up corporate risk, buffering companies from business cycles and market uncertainties on the home front. Most contingent workers in the United States are minorities, females, or uneducated males—a mirror image of third world contingents. Globalization places domestic contingents in competition with foreign workers, so that together they function as a worldwide peripheral labor market—the global equivalent of what Marx described as "the reserve army of labor."[22]

Globalization, along with rapid technological change, also drives the downsizing that is bringing new anxieties—and a new experience of economic wilding—to the American middle class. The 1990s became known as the Decade of Downsizing, with mass firings in more than half of the Fortune 500 firms. Many of these firms were profitable when they downsized and jacked up the pay of their executives as they were laying off workers. As noted in the last chapter, AT&T laid off 70,000 workers at the same time that CEO Bob Allen announced a multimillion-dollar pay increase for himself. *Business Week* ran a cover story called "Corporate Hit Men," with mug shots of Allen and three other like-minded CEOs on the cover, confirming the obvious wilding dimension of their greedy behavior.[23]

Respected labor economist Audrey Freedman told the *New York Times* in 1993 that downsizing "is going to be a permanent condition" and that "there are almost no long-term secure jobs" left in America.[24] Freedman's predictions are being borne out by a huge new wave of downsizing in the first years of the twenty-first century. In September 2000, Daimler-Chrysler announced that it would lay off 26,000 workers, one-fourth of its total global workforce. At about the same time, Lucent Technologies announced 16,000 new layoffs. A few months later, Nortel Networks and Verizon Communications announced 10,000 layoffs each. Motorola announced 9,370 layoffs, and Coca-Cola reported it would lay off 20 percent of its workers worldwide.

By mid-2001, large layoffs were proceeding in virtually every industry, from manufacturing to media giants to defense contractors, banks, and health care organizations. Downsizing has become the way that corporations signal to Wall Street that they are putting profit above all else, and Wall Street typically rewards big corporate downsizers with buy signals and higher stock prices. Among the other famous companies announcing major layoffs between 1999 and 2001 were AOL-Time Warner, Microsoft, Amazon.com, Lockheed Martin, Disney, BankAmerica, ExxonMobil, Chase, Boeing, Fleet Bank, Quaker Oats, Dell Computer, Ames Department Stores, United Technologies, Qwest Communications, Goodyear Tire and Rubber, JCPenney—the list is endless. Many of these companies are simply continuing years of chronic downsizing; ExxonMobil, for example, has now eliminated 238,000 of the 361,000 jobs it had in 1982. Moreover, ExxonMobil, BankAmerica, and many others—following AT&T's lead—have increased CEO pay by millions of dollars during layoffs. Such blatant greed by CEOs, whose incomes now are more than 400 times those of the average worker, has led even many shareholders to cry foul. Shareholders at BankAmerica and ExxonMobil have introduced new resolutions to prevent CEOs from massively raising their pay while laying off thousands of their own employees.

Downsizing has spread now to the dot-com world—and it is not a pretty picture. On Valentine's Day 2001, Collaborative Media, an online site run out of San Francisco, announced a layoff of 101 employees. The downsized dot-commers were shocked, having had no prior notification. When dismissed, they learned that they would not get paid for the last 10 days of their employment. "People feel as if they have been betrayed, that they have been lied to and that the company used them," said Tim Lefkowicz, former vice president who also missed his last paycheck. Downsizing at Internet companies surged in 2000, with more than 50,000 jobs eliminated. "They are young, smart and bitter," writes Jennifer Lee, who interviewed many of the casualties. "Many of them cannot believe," she writes, how cruel and "clumsy their former employers were in delivering the bad news."[25]

Downsizing has always been brutal for both casualties and survivors. For many of those with long years of service to a firm, it is not only an economic catastrophe but a Durkheimian wilding blow with severe anomic consequences. In the early 1990s, IBM was the biggest downsizer, announcing 85,000 cutbacks. Thousands of IBM employees had signed onto the company because of its promise of lifetime job security. Having devoted their lives to the corporate community, they had reason to feel morally betrayed when the company—which had taught them corporate loyalty as the highest value—unilaterally broke the covenant.

At Digital Equipment Corporation, another computer giant torn apart by massive downsizings in the 1990s, pink slips (notices that you are fired) arrived on Friday afternoons, leaving only a couple of hours to clear off one's desk. One laid-off employee reported that as he walked back to his office to collect his belongings, long-time colleagues scooted into their cubicles without meeting his eyes. None came to say goodbye. They feared, he said, that the pink slip was contagious, a kind of corporate AIDS virus.

Survivors of downsizing report a climate of terror in many companies. A Connecticut telephone company, for example, had maintained a no-layoff policy for 90 years but in the past decade initiated a series of downsizings, which are now commonplace in the communications industry. After the first wave of layoffs, the company "combined departments and then started chopping them off." Survivors, constantly at risk of losing their jobs, were continuously given new work assignments, adding stress and burnout to survivor guilt. "The panic and fear," one survivor said, was "so thick you could cut it with a knife."[26]

Underlying the downsizing panic is a new mortal threat to the American working and middle classes, which were created through a social contract delivering long-term, well-paying jobs. The contract, which partially kept at bay capitalism's egoistic and anomic tendencies, was ratified in New Deal legislation of the 1930s and reinforced in labor agreements and social welfare legislation through the 1960s following a century of dedicated labor and social struggles. But globalization has opened the door to a quick, corporate unburdening of the contract's good wages, expensive benefits, and long-term loyalty. As more and more corporations violate the contract, capitalism reverts to its earlier egoistic and anomic impulses, now played out by multinational robber barons on a global scale.

The collapse of the social contract is marked by the downsizing of entire core American industries and the rise of a new, anomic postindustrial economy. As GM, Ford, and Chrysler made record profits from their Mexican production plants and their entry into the aircraft, oil, and financial services businesses, half a million American autoworkers were abandoned. They have been joined in purgatory by millions of other displaced workers from textile, steel, and other industries fleeing to plants out of the country. Offered neither significant new training nor a viable safety net, many workers remain permanently unemployed or underemployed, forced into contract and temporary jobs or into low-paid service work without the protections and benefits that had been their ticket to the American Dream. This abandonment of the American working class by both government and corporate America is a spectacular variant of economic wilding and a moral barometer of capitalism without a social contract.

The new, futuristic postindustrial American economy—made up of high-tech multinational giants in communications, computers, finance, entertainment, and medical services—is, ironically, a throwback to the anomic capitalism of earlier times. High-tech corporate regions such as California's Silicon Valley have been described by both employees and researchers as dysfunctional contingent worlds, marked by ruthless competitiveness and profiteering, rootlessness, high turnover, astonishing disloyalty, and relatively invisible forms of exploitation and stratification. Supporting the highly paid computer entrepreneurs, electronic engineers, systems analysts, and hot-shot programmers—described by one scholar as a class of anomic loners who flit restlessly from one company to another in pursuit of the best deal—is a global network of contingent computer-assembly-line workers, from Mexico and Southeast Asia to far-flung areas of the United States. Their low wages, job insecurity, and often-dangerous work with poisonous chemicals or eye-straining electronic microscopes reflect the grim realities of contingent capitalism. Although the computer professionals and the assembly workers are at the polar extremes of the new postindustrial economy, neither enjoys the benefits of the old social contract, which more effectively preserved loyalty and community in a capitalist world.[27]

The Global Casino: Wilding on Wall Street

In defense of big corporations, it is true that they are driven by forces somewhat beyond their own control. Wall Street—and other global money markets where corporate stock is bought and sold—is even greedier than the companies. Investors want to see higher profits every quarter, and they will severely punish corporations that do not deliver.

Global financial markets have become the masters of the universe. Corporations cannot refuse their demands for short-term returns, and even most nations must bend to their will. Trillions of dollars each day swirl around the world chasing the best deal on new corporate issues, currency bets, pork bellies, or day trades. Increasingly such paper transactions, divorced from any concern with the well-being of workers, companies, or nations, are transforming the global economy into what seems a giant planetary casino.[28]

A high percentage of the activities in the financial markets are purely speculative, with respected financiers such as George Soros acknowledging that they are engaging in a form of high-stakes legalized gambling. Soros made more than a billion dollars in one day when he correctly predicted the movement of the British pound against the dollar. He is honest enough to say that speculators like himself often act as "legal outlaws" who manipulate money markets without regard to social consequences. The 1998 "Asian flu"—a huge financial crisis that is still crippling Thailand, South Korea, and many other Asian countries—was a product of uninhibited global financial wilding. Speculators poured trillions into the region for quick profit, then speculated against local currencies when loans went bad, forcing interest rates in the affected countries up so high that a ripple of bankruptcies spread across the whole continent. Speculators then pulled their money out fast, leaving millions unemployed and entire national economies in ruins.

Similar forms of financial wilding are helping drive the global search for sweatshops and are a major cause of corporate downsizing at home. As noted above, corporations downsize today to reassure investors that they are putting profits first, even at the expense of their workers. The markets typically reward such companies handsomely, with bigger layoffs bringing high praise on Wall Street. Hurting workers has become a prime corporate strategy for inflating stock prices.[29]

Sociologist Michael Useem writes of a new "investor capitalism" in which corporations are whipsawed by "impatient capital." Impatient capital—funds that are traded very quickly—is just another term for institutionalized greed in the money markets. The markets—driven by very wealthy individual investors as well as big institutional investors such as mutual and pension funds—have no patience for long-term strategies. As short-term greed intensifies, the entire global financial market moves toward a mode of institutionalized day trading, with investor-gamblers frantically shifting their investments around the world—aided by the lightning speed of the Internet.

Wall Street analysts who work at Merrill Lynch, Goldman Sachs, and other big investment banks become king-makers. Their buy and sell recommendations broadcast on MSNBC or other 24-hour business cable stations can make or break huge companies. Corporate behavior is increasingly directed toward shaping the perception of the analysts, whose judgments then shape the perceptions of the entire universe of investors. Financial markets have always been about manipulated perceptions and greed, and financial markets have always had some resemblance to casinos. But in the new financial environment that Federal Reserve chief Alan Greenspan has characterized as "irrational exuberance," the markets become a form of con game. Companies manipulate their financial statements to impress analysts and investors; analysts manipulate investor perceptions to further the interests of their own companies.[30]

A new scandal broke out in 2000 and 2001 that hints at institutionalized wilding by the Wall Street analysts who sit right at the center of the financial action. Investors rely on them for independent assessments of companies—from GM and GE to Microsoft and Intel—whose stock they want to buy or sell. But as *Sixty Minutes* and other television programs pointed out, the big Wall Street companies such as Merrill Lynch or Morgan Stanley Dean Witter, who employ the analysts, could depend for their own profits on doing business with the very companies that the analysts are profiling. The analysts, then, are understandably reluctant to make bearish recommendations about companies that their own employers are doing deals with—and, in fact, have incentives to inflate their forecasts. Put simply, analysts whose objectivity the public depends on may have to become sophisticated con artists to protect their jobs. Meanwhile, corporations are participating in the ruse by feeding analysts artificially reduced expectations that they can "exceed" at the end of the quarter, thus furthering the perception among investors and the public that they are doing better than the analysts expected.

The investing public is wising up to the problem, moving toward more independent amateur analysts on the Internet. Much buzz on Wall Street today is about "whisper numbers," those put out on the amateur Web sites. While the whisper numbers were off by 21 percent in a Bloomberg study, the Wall Street analysts were off by 44 percent. As financial journalist Michael Lewis writes, "The reason the amateurs now held the balance of power in the market was that they were, on average, more than twice as accurate as the pros—this in spite of the fact that the entire financial system was rigged in favor of the pros. The big companies spoon-fed their scoops directly to the pros; the amateurs were flying by radar."[31]

But even the amateurs are infected by their own greed and wilding fever. Young Jonathan Lebed, the 16-year-old suburban high school student who made hundreds of thousands of dollars promoting stock on the Internet, proved accurate in many of his predictions. Lebed, however, was in such a hurry to get rich that he ended up allegedly breaking laws regulating stock promotion, and distributing information about stocks from a con man who was telephoning numbers out from jail. Lebed's view of the markets was cynical but on target: "Whether it is analysts, brokers, advisers, Internet traders or the companies, everybody is manipulating the market. If it wasn't for everybody manipulating the market, there wouldn't be a stock market."[32]

Corporate Criminals Abroad
and At Home

Much of the economic wilding described in earlier sections—whether running global sweatshops, downsizing profitable companies, or inflating stock estimates—is perfectly legal. While the new legal wilding is the most important and disturbing trend, another trend is global corporate criminality. The crimes show how far most big companies are now prepared to go to secure and sustain big profits.

On August 9, 2000, Bridgestone/Firestone of Japan recalled 6.5 million tires in the United States, citing the danger of rollovers and tire separations that could lead to fatal accidents. But the sequence of events suggested that the company was covering up deadly deceit. At least 88 motorists had already been killed in accidents, and inquiries by journalists and Congress would show that the company had had evidence much earlier that the tires were defective and dangerous.

An internal memorandum from Ford, whose Explorer SUVs were often involved, showed that in 1999 Bridgestone/Firestone had opposed a tire recall from Saudi Arabia because of fear that it might be reported to U.S. regulators. This initial hint of deceit is reinforced by disclosures that Bridgestone/Firestone had been briefed much earlier about the rising costs of tire-related insurance or warranty claims of property damage, personal injury, and death. As Alabama Republican Senator Richard Shelby said, "Ford and Firestone had at a minimum a moral obligation to make sure that the products they sell to the American public and other people in other countries are safe. And yet they both failed to bring this issue to consumers' and the federal government's attention, at the cost of dozens of lives, I am afraid."[33]

While the Bridgestone/Firestone case is emerging as one of the biggest product liability scandals in years, globalization limits corporate vulnerability. In Venezuela, for example, where more than 60 deaths were reported on highways, there is minimal consumer protection. There is no class-action suit concept in the law and no network of consumer lawyers and advocates to advance the case. While the Venezuelan government recommended that criminal action be taken against both Bridgestone/Firestone and Ford, the lack of a consumer protection tradition makes the case problematic, as does the overwhelming money and legal talent that the companies have to bring to any potential court fight.[34]

The pattern of deceit by Bridgestone/Firestone evokes another of the most infamous economic wilding cases of recent memory, which led to far more deaths. The case broke in the 1990s when Jeffrey Wigand, an executive at tobacco giant Brown and Williamson, revealed documents showing that the major cigarette companies had covered up evidence for years showing that smoking was addictive and caused cancer. Since then, tobacco executives have acknowledged the coverup but shifted their marketing toward poor nations where public health regulations and consumer laws are minimal.

The conspiracy by Philip Morris and the other major tobacco firms led to 12 million deaths from smoking from 1964 to 1998. A Brown and Williamson document from the 1960s, 40 years before the companies admitted the fact, said flatly: "We are, then, in the business of selling nicotine, an addictive drug." David Kessler, former chief of the Food and Drug Administration, showed that the companies deliberately reengineered the cigarette over many years to be a pure nicotine-delivery system. Meanwhile, adhering to a script followed religiously for decades, the companies suppressed evidence, always denied the addiction and cancer claims as unprovable, and intensified their marketing to children and foreigners. The unspeakable magnitude of the crime helps explain the unprecedented $144-billion class-action award against the companies made in 2000 by a Florida jury.[35]

Russell Mokhiber and Robert Weissman, editors of *Multi-National Monitor* and authors of the recent book *Corporate Predators,* are the great muckrakers of today's corporate crime. Each year, they publish the *Monitor*'s "10 worst corporations of the year," a graphic list of corporate intrigue, violence, and sedition that is true crime at its best. Whether reporting on the French oil company El Aquitaine's alleged coup in the Congo to depose an uncooperative president, U.S. coal mining companies that cheat on air quality reports as coal miners die of black lung disease, or Tyson Food's illegal political donations, they show that criminality has become standard operating procedure for the world's biggest companies.[36]

Mokhiber and Weissman have compiled a new list of the "top 100 corporate criminals" of the 1990s. In their introduction, they note that street crime costs the United States $3.8 billion a year, while corporate fraud in just one industry—health care—costs Americans $100 billion to $400 billion each year. They also note that for every reported corporate crime, hundreds of others are not reported or prosecuted; they also note that the companies being prosecuted are the same ones that—through campaign financing, lobbying, and other political influence—increasingly write the laws governing their own industries.

The list itself is a *Who's Who* of the world's great companies. Among the top 10 corporate criminals are pharmaceutical giant Hoffmann-LaRoche, convicted in 1999 of antitrust activities and slapped with a half-billion dollar fine; Exxon, convicted for environmental offenses; Bankers Trust, for financial fraud; and Archer Daniels Midlands, for antitrust activities. The top 100 include Pfizer, Rockwell, Northrop, Eastman Chemical, GE, ConAgra, Blue Cross, Adolph Coors, United States Sugar, International Paper, E-Systems, and Teledyne Industries. All paid fines for convictions, and six—including Exxon, Rockwell, Warner-Lambert, Teledyne, and United Technologies—each pled guilty to more than one crime in the 1990s.

Mokhiber and Weissman will have to hire more helpers to keep up with corporate crime in the new century. In 2000 and 2001, prosecutors are seeing a huge new wave of crimes in the pharmaceutical, securities, airline, defense, telecommunications, and other major industries. The new prosecution of tobacco companies for smuggling cigarettes into Canada suggests that corporate wilders are recidivists who are not about to be deterred by years of prosecution and class-action suits. With more money and lawyers than the government or consumers have, they seem to have concluded that crime pays.

Globalization without Wilding: The Future of Globalization after the Battle of Seattle

In December 1999, the streets of Seattle became a fiery battleground with U.S. tanks on the streets, Nike windows shattered, and tear gas shots heard around the world. Fifty thousand protesters—many of them college students teaming up with workers and environmentalists ("Teamsters for Turtles")—rallied to shut down the meeting of the World Trade Organization (WTO). Their goal was not to end globalization but to challenge the WTO—which helps make the rules of the global economy—to make new rules protecting human rights as well as protecting money.

Seattle was a Constitutional Moment, a recognition that financial elites from the richest nations are making basic rules that will determine how the world is run for decades to come. The protesters, who want globalization without wilding, have shown their determination; they have mounted electrifying protests since Seattle at nearly every meeting of the financial elites who make the rules—from Washington in April 2000, to Prague in September 2000, to Davos, Switzerland, in January 2001, to Quebec City in April 2001. As the corporate elites look for places to meet in quiet secrecy, choosing in 2001 to hold the next WTO meeting in the desert of Quatar, a Mideast dictatorship, the protesters defy efforts to deter them with police violence and armed fortifications. In Davos, many protesters actually skied in to evade blockades at the border and on the streets.

As noted at the beginning of this chapter, globalization could be organized in a different way to reap the benefits of global specialization, production, and trade without inflicting harm on millions of the world's workers and communities. Why, then, have our political leaders allowed globalization to proceed in its current form? And how might the global economy be restructured and regulated to balance the enormous power of multinational corporations and contain their greed?

The United States will retain significant influence in the new web of global institutions, from the International Monetary Fund (IMF) and the World Bank to the World Trade Association. But the players gaining the most power in the new world economy are not the governments of the United States and other nations, but the multinationals themselves. The reason for the acquiescence of both Republican and Democratic presidents to their agenda is simple: Both political parties are dependent upon business funding to win elections and are not prepared to risk opposing huge global corporations on issues of central importance to them. Five hundred of the largest U.S. corporations have offices in Washington and employ thousands of lobbyists, as do 400 of the largest foreign multinationals, together constituting by far the largest and most influential special-interest group in Washington. Ultimately, business sets the parameters for economic policymaking in America, because members of the U.S. corporate elite themselves occupy the highest governmental economic posts, and because they control the money and investment decisions essential to the survival of both the population and the government.[37]

Students and other Seattle protesters have already shown that their actions can force change. The protests in 2000 and 2001 have triggered a major crisis among the financial elites, with corporations rushing to embrace an image of social responsibility. The president of the World Bank, James Wolfensohn, claims that he is now moving his agency to focus on the needs of the global poor. The U.S. government has pulled back some of its support for institutions such as the IMF and indicated a concern with introducing labor and environmental rights in trade agreements.

The aim of the protesters is to turn globalization into a means of empowering people and dignifying their lives. One approach is to promote global labor movements to represent the interests of the new global workforce and balance the power of the multinationals. Both American workers and employees in developing nations need strong unions to prevent the horrendous exploitation of global sweatshops and contingent employment. But the U.S. government has avoided any identification with American unions and has done nothing to support the embryonic movement for independent unions in Mexico, Indonesia, and other developing countries. President George W. Bush, with a long anti-labor record, is unlikely to pursue even the small steps that President Clinton took to promote unions and labor rights around the world, including the effort to introduce provisions for worker and environmental rights into NAFTA and at WTO negotiations.

American unions are starting to develop new international strategies. U.S. unions now realize that when we allow corporations to operate sweatshops abroad, U.S. workers will begin to encounter sweatshop conditions at home. After years of hostility to foreign workers and labor movements, the AFL-CIO U.S. labor chiefs have begun to speak about international labor solidarity and to put their money where their mouths are. John Sweeney, current head of the U.S. labor movement, has provided vocal support and funding for organizing efforts in the *maquiladoras* and other trade zones. As early as 1994, workers in a Ford truck-assembly plant in St. Paul, Minnesota, voted to send funds to Ford workers in Mexico to support a union drive in the *maquiladoras*. The American workers, who recognized that wretched Mexican wages and working conditions affected their own jobs and security, wore patches on their jackets saying "Cross-Border Solidarity Organizers." A growing number of labor unions—such as the U.S. United Electrical Workers, with help from the Teamsters—have begun to contribute to independent labor organizing in the *maquiladoras*.[38]

The rise of new international labor confederations—in coalition with student groups, environmentalists, and other human rights groups—could help prevent multinationals from playing one country's workers against another's in a race to the bottom. It could also help create new controls over the unchecked lightning-fast movement of speculative capital around the planet. As the Asian crisis of 1998 showed, such fast money can easily destabilize the economies of entire continents and erode the ability of nations to protect their own people. We need foreign investment and trade, but only when there are speed-bumps and checks that allow nations and communities to control their own destinies.[39]

Ultimately, a new democratic coalition must become a major player at the tables where the new constitution of the global economy is being written. The finance ministers of the rich nations and the corporate advisory teams who meet regularly at the WTO, IMF, and World Bank will have to make room for a whole new set of worker and citizen representatives. Global rules will have to shift from their exclusive focus on protecting property rights and free trade. The new mission is creating a democratic model of globalization, centered on respect for human rights and a fair distribution of wealth between rich and poor nations, as well as between corporate CEOs and their global workforce.[40]

This may seem a long, steep climb, but one immediate step along the way is to build up codes of international labor standards and corporate conduct that would set a humane global floor for wages and working conditions. The European Union has established a European Social Charter setting minimum wages, health and safety standards, and other social codes to be honored by all the member nations. The International Labor Organization (ILO) also has a code of global labor rights that now needs to be toughened and enforced in all nations and corporations, with sanctions imposed on companies that wild by ignoring the codes. Although President Clinton negotiated NAFTA with side agreements to protect labor and the environment, most observers saw them as pitifully weak. Citizen and labor groups are pushing for far stronger agreements consistent with or stronger than current United Nations and ILO standards as well as a robust social charter for *maquiladora* businesses.[41]

Apparel companies such as Nike, Reebok, and Wal-Mart have banded together in the Fair Labor Association to form their own corporate codes of conduct, promising to avoid use of child labor or prison labor and to pay the prevailing wages in each country in which they operate. Such corporate codes across an entire sector are an important first step to end corporate wilding. But it will take public action to make the companies accountable and truly end the new wave of global economic wilding. Students in the anti-sweatshop movement have proved that even huge, ruthless companies such as Nike can be forced to change by consumer boycotts. Across the nation, students in 2000 and 2001 have become more careful about their own buying habits and mounted visible boycotts at Nike stores that have helped change Nike policy. They have also forced their universities to break ties with companies that continue to operate sweatshops around the world and helped create new monitoring and enforcement agencies to ensure that the companies do not continue to wild on the sly.[42]

Multinational companies in the United States and elsewhere have used globalism to escape their social responsibilities and weaken the accountability that the workers and governments of their own nations have historically imposed on them. This will lead to a permanent regime of corporate wilding unless a new social covenant is negotiated between multinationals and the workers and citizens of the world. Building a new world community through the struggle for global employee rights and democratic and accountable multinational corporations may prove the most important new social movement of the coming era.

Notes

1. "Made in the USA?" 2001. National Labor Committee, New York, February 12, (Published on the Internet).
2. Herbert, Bob. 1994. "Terror In Toyland." *New York Times*, December 21, p. A27.
3. For a concise, readable interpretation of globalization as a "race to the bottom," see Brecher, Jeremy and Tim Costello. 1998. *Global Village or Global Pillage?* 2d ed. Boston: South End Press.
4. Kernaghan, Charles. (2000). "Made in China: Behind the Label." New York: National Labor Committee.
5. Brown, Sherrod. 2001. "Pentagon Sweatshops." *The Progressive*, February, pp. 31–32.
6. Barnet, Richard and John Cavanaugh. 1994. *Global Dreams*. New York: Simon & Schuster, pp. 321ff. See also Fuentes, Annette and Barbara Ehrenreich. 1992. *Women in the Global Factory*. Boston: South End Press, pp. 10ff.
7. La Botz, Dan. 1992. *Mask of Democracy: Labor Suppression in Mexico Today*. Boston: South End Press, p. 162.
8. International Labor Rights Fund. 2001. "Report to Universities Regarding the Kukdong International Conflict in Axtlico, Puebla, Mexico" Report on Internet, January 25. Worker Rights Consortium. 2001. Letter to Nike, Scott Nova (WRC Executive Director), January 14.
9. Dillon, Sam. 2001. "Profits Raise Pressure on Border Factories." *New York Times*, February 15, pp. A1, A9.
10. La Botz, *Mask of Democracy*, p. 164.
11. Ibid., pp. 164–68.
12. Thompson, Ginger. 2001. "Chasing Mexico's Dream into Squalor." *New York Times*, February 11, pp. A1, A8.
13. Ibid.
14. Barnet and Cavanaugh, *Global Dreams*, p. 303.
15. Greenhouse, Steven. 2001. "2 Clothing Factories Accused of Forced, Unpaid Overtime." *New York Times*, February 12, p. A24.
16. Ibid.

17. Barnet and Cavanaugh, *Global Dreams*, p. 333; "Sweatshops Flourish a Century after Their Danger Was Detailed." 1995. *New York Times*, February 6, pp. A1, B4.
18. See Derber, Charles. 2000. *Corporation Nation*. New York: St. Martin's Press, Chap. 5.
19. Belous, Richard S. 1989. *The Contingent Economy: The Growth of the Temporary, Part-Time and Subcontracted Workforce*. (Washington, DC: National Planning Association.) For further discussion of the contradictions, see Derber, Charles. 1994. "Clintradictions." *Tikkun* 9(5): 15ff.
20. Quotations from contingent workers in this paragraph and below are drawn from interview transcripts of a study of temporary workers in Boston carried out by the author in 1994.
21. For a discussion of the relation between globalization and contingent work, see Harrison, Bennett. 1994. *Lean and Mean: The Changing Landscape of Corporate Power in the Age of Flexibility*. New York: Basic Books, chap. 9.
22. For a useful discussion of the relation between contingency and risk, see Osnowitz, Debra. 1995. "Contingent Work as Risky Business." Unpublished manuscript, Dept. of Sociology, Brandeis University, Waltham, MA.
23. For an in-depth discussion of downsizing, see Derber, *Corporation Nation*.
24. Cited in Kilborn, Peter. 1993. "New Jobs Lack the Old Security in a Time of Disposable Workers." *New York Times*, March 15, p. C1.
25. Lee, Jennifer. 2001. "Discarded Dreams of Dot-Com Rejects." *New York Times*, February 21, pp. C1, C8.
26. Quotes of downsizing victims are drawn from the study of temporary workers cited in note 20.
27. See Harrison, *Lean and Mean*, chaps. 5, 8, and 9.
28. Korten, David. 1999. *The Post-Corporate World*. San Francisco: Berrett Koehler Press; Derber, *Corporation Nation*.
29. Derber, *Corporation Nation*, chap. 5.
30. Ibid.
31. Lewis, Michael. 2001. "Jonathan Lebed's Extracurricular Activities." *New York Times Magazine*, February 25, p. 33.
32. Ibid., p. 32.
33. Wald, Matthew L. and Keith Bradsher. 2000. "More Indications Hazards of Tires Were Long Known." *New York Times*, September 6, p. A1; Wald, Matthew L. and Keith Bradsher. 2000. "Questions on Tire-Defect Data Arise as Hearings Draw Near." *New York Times*, September 5, p. C1.
34. Rohter, Larry. 2000. "Low-Profile Consumer Protection: Experts See Venezuela Ill-Equipped to Deal with Tire Debacle." *New York Times*, September 8, p. C1.

35. Kessler, David. 2001. *A Question of Intent: A Great American Battle with a Deadly Industry*. New York: Public Affairs.
36. Mokhiber, Russell and Robert Weissman. 1999. *Corporate Predators*. Monroe, ME: Common Courage Press.
37. Barnet and Cavanaugh, *Global Dreams*. See also Phillips, Kevin. 1994. *Arrogant Capital*. Boston: Little, Brown, chap. 1.
38. Brecher and Costello, *Global Village or Global Pillage?*
39. Derber, *Corporation Nation,* chap. 14; Brecher, Jeremy, Tim Costello, and Brendan Smith. 2000. *Globalization from Below*. Boston: South End Press.
40. Brecher and Costello, *Global Village or Global Pillage?*
41. Derber, *Corporation Nation.*
42. Ibid.

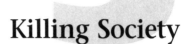

Killing Society

The Ungluing of America

A nation never falls but by suicide.

—Ralph Waldo Emerson

An American Dream that does not spell out the moral consequences of unmitigated self-interest threatens to turn the next generation of Americans into wilding machines. In a pattern already visible today, Americans could turn not only on each other but on society as well, too self-absorbed to make the commitments and observe the moral constraints that hold stable communities together. There is already abundant evidence that a wilder generation of Americans is assaulting and abandoning society, allowing the guarantees of civilized behavior and the most vital social institutions to languish and die as this generation pursues its own selfish dreams.

The breakdown of society that I describe in this chapter—from violence on the streets to state violence, from broken schools to a broken politics—is a cause as well as a consequence of the wilding crisis. The wilding culture poisons families, workplaces, and neighborhoods, which in their weakened form are fertile spawning grounds for more wilding. There is no first cause in this chicken-and-egg causal chain; the wilding virus creates social breakdown and simultaneously grows out of it.

Wilding in the Streets

America's culture of wilding, at its extreme, is triggering an epidemic of bizarre and terrifying violence. The new violence constitutes a direct assault on society, threatening the social infrastructure that sustains civilized life.

On February 1, 2001, police arrested a 9-year-old boy who allegedly attacked four of his schoolmates with a hypodermic needle. Running through the gymnasium in Public School 66 in Brooklyn, New York, he reportedly stabbed two boys and two girls, who had to be rushed to the hospital.[1] A yet more bizarre needle attack took place on New York City streets some years earlier, when 10 teenage girls were arrested and "charged with jabbing women with pins in dozens of unprovoked attacks on the Upper West Side over a one-week period." The girls "thought it was fun to run down Broadway," Deputy Police Chief Ronald Fenrich said, and stick "women with pins to see their reactions." The girls expressed some remorse, Fenrich said, although mainly "they were sorry they got caught." Meanwhile, the neighborhood residents, although they had seen more vicious crimes, told reporters that they found the pinprick attacks an "intolerable invasion, both because of the cavalier manner in which the attacks were carried out, and because rumors spread early that it was possible the jabs had come from AIDS-infected needles."[2]

American cities have always been violent places, but the pinprick attacks are emblematic of a new, more menacing violence and a more profound breakdown of social life. Like the expressive wilding in Central Park, it involves taking pleasure in the inflicting of pain and complete indifference to the sensibilities of the victims. For the potential targets—anyone walking the street—the message is to remain hypervigilant and assume that every pedestrian is a potential threat.

The horrifying image of children killing children has helped define our era. In February 2001, a Florida jury convicted Lionel Tate, 12, of first-degree murder for killing a 6-year-old girl while practicing wrestling moves he had seen on television. Just two weeks later, Massachusetts police arrested an 11-year-old boy for stabbing another boy to death in a Springfield movie theater. Less than two years earlier, a 10-year-old Massachusetts boy was charged with murdering a 5-week-old baby.

The epidemic of kids murdering kids first grabbed public attention in the 1990s. In October 1994 two Chicago boys, aged 10 and 11, threw a 5-year-old child, Erik Morris, to his death from a 14th-floor window. The reason: Erik had refused to steal candy for them. Erik's 8-year-old brother had desperately tried to save him but was overpowered by the bigger boys.

A month earlier, Chicagoan Robert Sandifer, aged 11, was killed by two boys, aged 14 and 16, who feared that Sandifer would squeal about their gang activities to police. Sandifer, shortly before his own murder, had killed a 14-year-old girl, Shavan Dean, when he fired a volley of bullets into a group of teenagers playing football. Young Sandifer was buried with his teddy bear.

Violent crime throughout the United States peaked in the mid-1990s, but rates of murder, armed burglary, and other violent crimes remain exceptionally high—far higher than in Western European nations, Japan, and other developed countries. A survey of 10,000 youths aged 12 to 17, released in November 2000, documents that violence is rampant. Funded by 18 federal agencies, the study reports that one out of four students, representing about 5.3 million American children, "told investigators they had either used a gun or knife, carried such a weapon or had been involved in an incident in which someone was injured by a weapon in the past year." Robert Blum, the principal researcher, concluded that "the prevalence of violence is much higher than we expected, particularly when you consider we've taken out all the fistfighting that seventh- and eighth-grade boys do." He might have added that the study also factored out the violence rates among the astonishing number of young people whom we have locked up in federal and state prisons.[3]

School violence is now widely considered a national crisis in itself. On February 29, 2000, a 6-year-old child allegedly fired a .32-caliber pistol at a 6-year-old girl in a classroom at Buell Elementary School near Flint, Michigan. According to eyewitnesses, the boy tucked the gun in his pants, pulled it out, and fired, striking her in the neck. He then reportedly ran into a nearby bathroom and threw the gun into a trash can. The girl, Kayla Rolland, died 30 minutes later. According to one report, the motive might have arisen out of a scuffle between the two on the playground the day before.[4]

The U.S. Center for Disease Control reports that almost 10 percent of children bring a weapon to school. School violence peaked in the early 1990s, but incidents with multiple fatalities have increased, the most famous being the 1999 massacre at Columbine High School in Littleton, Colorado. At Columbine, two students in black trench coats opened fire with semiautomatic machine guns inside the school and killed 15 people, with a total of 20 injured. As in many of these incidents, the motives for this expressive wilding involved jealousy and revenge for being excluded from the most popular circles—the rage of the outcast. But they also mirrored the violent culture of the school that they hated. Columbine put the toughest football players on a pedestal, honoring physical force. The Columbine area also has a strong military presence, and the young killers had grown up infatuated with war and surrounded by guns.

The chronicle of school violence in the last decade is stupefying. On December 6, 1999, a 13-year-old student in Fort Gibson, Oklahoma, came to school and shot at least four of his classmates with his father's 9-mm semiautomatic weapon. A few weeks earlier, a 12-year-old boy in a Deming, New Mexico, middle school shot and killed a female classmate, aged 12, in the schoolyard. On May 15, 1998, a 15-year-old student in Springfield, Ohio, killed two classmates in the school cafeteria. On May 21, 1998, police reported that three sixth-grade boys had a "hit list" and had been plotting to kill many of their classmates in a sniper attack at school during a false fire alarm. A few months earlier, in a high school in West Paducah, Kentucky, a 14-year-old student killed three students and wounded five others while they were participating in a prayer circle in a school hallway. And a few months before that, a 16-year-old student in Pearl, Mississippi, shot and killed his mother and then shot nine students at school.[5]

Children themselves are terrified in many schools and neighborhoods. Fourteen-year-old Chirll Rivers is a Boston student who says she's scared: "I don't want to die. You have to watch your back every day. Someone could mistake you for someone else and shoot you. I could be the wrong person."[6] Another kid, forced to walk home from a youth program after a van broke down, collapsed in a panic, crying, "I can't walk home, I just can't walk home. Someone got killed on my street. I'll get killed too." The *Boston Globe* reported that this youth did get home, running all the way, but that in the next eight days, three young men did not have the same luck—killed on the same street—while a fourth was fatally shot through the window of his mother's apartment. The result of this unprecedented epidemic of violence, the *Globe* said, was that "increasing numbers of city youths are arming themselves, carrying small knives and pistols tucked into their waistbands or inside their coats."[7]

A new wave of school violence erupted in Boston schools in 2001, creating a crisis in the city. On January 19, 2001, a parent attacked a first-grade teacher, who was sent to the hospital with a black eye and fractured cheekbone. Within three weeks of this incident, an eighth-grader punched an assistant principal and a knife-wielding ninth-grader chased a track coach. A week later, assailants with knives stabbed boys in two different schools. According to the National Center for Education Statistics, despite a reduction in juvenile crime rates, the national percentage of students saying they felt too unsafe to go to school at least once per month grew to 5.2 percent in 1999, compared to 4 percent in 1997. And, according to another study released in 2001, a majority of U.S. teenagers used violence in the last year, and one in five boys brought a weapon to high school. "The seeds of violence," said Institute of Ethics President Michael Josephson, who funded the study, "can be found in schools all over America."[8]

Suburbs, Small Towns, and National Parks: New Wilding Terrains

It is not only city life that is being subverted by the new wilding. Columbine High, the new symbol of horrific school violence, is in the suburbs. So is Santana High School, where a 15-year-old boy, Charles "Andy"

Williams, allegedly killed 2 fellow students and wounded 13 others in a wild shooting spree on March 5, 2001. Santana High is in Santee, California, a middle-class suburb of San Diego. Williams, known as a "nice" and "sociable" kid, was into sports. Although some friends and parents said that Andy had been "picked on" by other kids, nobody saw him as a potential murderer, and few of the shocked suburbanites saw their town as a place where mass murder could happen. But the Santana High shooting was followed by a rash of new suburban school killings from California to Florida.[9]

The image of suburbs as a peaceful haven from city violence began to shatter almost a decade ago. In November 1994, six teenagers from Abington Township, a quiet, middle-class suburb of Philadelphia, went on their own wilding spree, savagely beating Eddie Polec, aged 16, to death with clubs and baseball bats. Law enforcement officials said this might have been part of a "fun outing," although there were reports that the murder was retaliation for the alleged rape of an Abington girl.

One Abington mother, expressing the shock of the community, said, "These are suburban kids—you don't figure them to go bad. It's not their character to be a rough group of kids." An Abington father and rabbi, Aaron Landes, said, "There was a presupposition we lived in a kind of safe cocoon because we lived in suburbia. There are many families who have struggled to buy a home in suburbia to avoid the urban ills for their children." But suburbs have become cauldrons of both street and domestic violence, including an explosion of child abuse and neglect cases among educated and professionally successful suburban parents.[10]

Priscilla Dillon, a social worker whose caseload is in Weston, Wellesley, and other posh suburbs of Boston, says that the frequency of suburban "family cris[e]s has escalated." The kids, she says, "act out the frustrations of the family by running away, drinking, doing drugs, confusion. The only difference is that they are not publicized as much as they are in the inner city." Suburban social workers say the suburban ethos of success triggers the problem. Some highly successful parents "are quite absent from their kids' emotional development" and others, who "have very, very high standards for their children," put "undue pressure" on them to replicate their parents' success. Other social workers say that neglected suburban kids are more likely to end up isolated than those in inner cities who find gangs to join. The rage of the lonely suburban kid produces a "Sampson complex"— the desire to commit suicide and bring everyone else down with you.[11]

Stephen Lutz, a 17-year-old student at Abington High, renamed "Murder High," aptly concluded: "Maybe we can learn violence is not a city thing. It's not a suburban thing. It's not an Abington thing. It's a society thing. It can touch you anywhere."[12]

Violent wilding has spread not only to suburbs but also to small towns. Robert Tulloch and James Parker, the teenagers accused of murdering two professors at Dartmouth in 2001, hail from Chelsea, Vermont, a town of about 1,000 people. The town, which has changed little in the last 40 years, is a picture-postcard New England community. "Everybody knows everybody," says John Upham, a longtime resident. Another resident, Robert Sherman, says that "nobody is invisible in Chelsea." Yet the Internet, where Tulloch and Parker spent much of their time and bought the knife that they allegedly used to stab the professors multiple times, drew the boys away from full integration into the community, possibly one factor explaining their alleged brutal violence.[13]

Despite the close-knit community existing in many such towns, signs of a wilding epidemic began popping up in the early 1990s, well before the Internet. In 1993, the small town of Ayer, Massachusetts, had a higher rate of aggravated assault than either Boston or Worcester, and in 1994 small towns in Massachusetts were experiencing the largest crime-rate increases in the state. In the new climate, the traditional friendliness of small towns, ironically, is becoming a spur to crime. In Kewanee, Illinois, a tiny, close community, Roger Harlow, a 48-year-old Sunday School teacher, was arrested and charged with more than 85 burglaries in December 1994, mostly in homes of his friends and business acquaintances. Harlow would invite friends out to lunch and arrive late after stopping to burglarize their homes. Darrell Johnson, a country club and Elks associate of Harlow, says, "I'm mad at myself, too, for leaving the house open. Not anymore."[14]

Even our national parks are becoming violent places. Paul Crawford, a park ranger who now wears a .357 magnum revolver on his hip alongside his bully club and handcuffs, says, "Fighting, stealing, killing, we get it all. People drop their guard when they come to the parks, and that's why the criminals follow them here." John C. Benjamin, a district ranger, agrees. "I thought I'd be out here protecting the environment," Benjamin says. "I had no idea I would be breaking up bar fights, investigating murders and making reports on assaults."[15]

National park officials in Washington have called for bulletproof vests for their rangers. "Things have gotten a lot more intense," says Robert C. Mariott. "It used to be that we'd run into a belligerent drunk occasionally. But now," continues Mariott, rangers routinely "run into people who are confrontational and violent." Ranger Robert L. McGhee was shot to death in Mississippi after "making a traffic stop on a park road." Drug rings have been uncovered in several national parks, and officials say that the parks have become stalking grounds for bands of thieves hunting automobiles, camera equipment, and jewelry.[16]

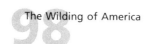

People come to national parks to restore their faith in society. A Detroit truck driver says one of the reasons he likes camping is that in the park he "can leave things in the tent. . . . It's not like the city, where you have to lock everything up." But Jenn DeRosa, a New Jerseyite who camped across the country with her friend Steve Grillo and had her bicycle, money, and all her credit cards stolen, today prepares for camping as if she were a hardened inner-city dweller. "I feel pretty safe," DeRosa says, because she now carries a knife.[17]

Domestic Violence Run Amok: Wilding in the Kitchen and the Bedroom

One of the remarkable things about Ik society is the complete unraveling of the family. Consumed by the desperate quest to get food, an Ik views family obligations as "insane." Family members, the Ik believe, are either "burdens" or competitors, in either case an obstacle to filling one's own stomach. The Ik are quick to cast off old parents and children, whom they view as "useless appendages." Bila, an unexceptional Ik mother, frequently took her baby to the fields, hoping a predator would take it away. When a leopard finally made off with it, she "was delighted. She was rid of the child and no longer had to carry it about and feed it."[18]

An extreme wilding culture spells death for the family, as it does for society as a whole. The family is ultimately a set of demanding social obligations and commitments, requiring a sense of moral obligation and a robust capacity to think beyond oneself.

America's own wilding culture seems at first blush to be reinforcing the family rather than subverting it. Wilding has made the outside world a dangerous place. To protect themselves, journalist Chris Black writes, "citizens have hunkered down with their nuclear families and turned their homes into suburban bunkers against the threats" outside. Sociologist Ray Oldenburg says that as the sense of community erodes and the city streets become scary, "we have replaced the ideal community with the ideal private home." Americans try to keep off the streets, spending time with family rather than friends, watching videos at home rather than venturing out to the movies. Marketing consultant Faith Popcorn calls the trend "cocooning"—escaping into the warm bosom of one's

own family and home in order to tune out the rest of the world. The family, in Christopher Lasch's phrase, beckons as the only "haven in a heartless world."[19]

Families, however, are always more a mirror of the outside world than a barrier against it, and wilding on the outside is helping to unglue the American family, turning it into an unstable and increasingly heartless haven. As Americans harden themselves to survive on the streets and compete at work, they make more conditional family commitments and may be becoming more indifferent to or violent toward the people to whom they are closest. Taking violence as one indicator, veteran researchers Richard J. Gelles and Murray A. Straus report: "The cruel irony of staying home because one fears violence in the streets is that the real danger of personal attack is in the home. Offenders are not strangers climbing through windows, but loved ones, family members."[20]

Approximately 5,000 Americans each year murder someone in their immediate family—about half of these killing a spouse and the other half, a parent, child, or sibling—accounting for almost 25 percent of all murders in the country. A staggering number of Americans are physically assaulted by family members each year, including more than 1.5 million elderly victims, more than 2 million children, and more than 2 million wives who are severely beaten by their husbands. In America a wife is beaten, the FBI estimates, every 30 seconds, and more than 40 percent of the most brutally beaten, according to researchers William Stacey and Anson Shupe, are pregnant at the time. The fantastic obsession with the O. J. Simpson case partly reflects the epidemic of expressive wilding in the form of spousal abuse that is poisoning America.

As for children and the elderly, the greatest threat comes not from strangers, the *Boston Globe* reports, "but overwhelmingly from their families," where new forms of abuse are on the rise. Despite all the publicity on TV and milk cartons about strangers snatching kids, the *Globe* notes, there are no more than 300 such cases a year, whereas there are now "more than 160,000 family abductions annually, and nearly 60,000 youngsters expelled from their homes and refused reentry." Typical of elderly victims, who get less public attention than battered spouses and abused or abandoned children, is a 77-year-old California woman who told police her son repeatedly "hit her on the head with beer bottles," a 71-year-old Massachusetts man who "suffered a six-inch gash in his forehead when his son struck him with a frying pan," and an 80-year-old California grandmother who was imprisoned by her grandsons. She was "isolated from all outside contact" while they cashed her Social Security checks and depleted her bank account.[21]

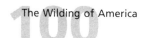
The Unglued Family: Divorce, Singles, and the Sociology of the Heart in the "Postmarital" Era

The American family is clearly becoming a less stable institution, the traditional bonds between spouses and between parents and children eroding so rapidly that some fear the nuclear family may not survive the new century. Former senator Daniel Patrick Moynihan, reviewing evidence that only 6 percent of black children and 30 percent of white children will grow up with both parents, says we are already in a "postmarital" society. "The scale of marital breakdown," writes historian Lawrence Stone, "has no historical precedent that I know of, and seems unique. There has been nothing like it for the last 2,000 years, and probably much longer."[22]

At least three long-term, unambiguous trends signal a dramatic ungluing of the family as we have known it: sustained high rates of divorce, a precipitous increase in the number of single-parent households, and an extraordinary increase in the numbers of Americans living outside any family structure. Demographer James R. Wetzel reports that divorce rates are now holding steady at double those "of the average of the 1950–1964 period, and about triple the average of the 1920s and 1930s." Wetzel estimates that "more than half of all marriages . . . will end in divorce." Among young people marrying today between the ages of 18 and 24, approximately 75 percent will divorce. Marriage is no longer "for better or for worse," but on average for about seven years, after which time a declining number of divorcees will remarry, with an even higher probability of divorcing again for those who do. This decisive breakdown in permanent relationships may be, as Stone suggests, the most important revolution of modern times, a "watershed in the culture of the West."[23]

The number of single-parent households is another revolutionary development. The number of single-parent families tripled from the 1950s to the 1990s. The number of single-parent families continues to grow and is about one-third the number of two-parent families.[24]

Perhaps the most dramatic signal of family unraveling is the number of Americans living outside any family system. "Families were the order of the day early in the twentieth century," Wetzel writes, and as late as

1940, only about 7.5 percent of Americans lived outside a family. To-day, almost 30 percent of households are made up of single or unrelated people and more than 30 million adult Americans now live alone.[25]

Family ungluing, particularly divorce, reflects some very important positive developments—such as the new freedom of economically in-dependent women to leave bad marriages. But it also reflects the most radical individualistic currents of the modern era, currents far more pow-erful in America than anywhere else. Traditional family obligations are becoming too confining for a growing segment of Americans. Lawrence Stone argues that since 1960 American "spouses are being traded in al-most as cheaply and easily as used cars," reflecting "a moral and cul-tural shift to untrammeled individualism." This is consistent with a long-term cultural revolution in which people withdraw some of their attachments to their communities in order to gain more freedom for themselves. As early as 1853, Horace Greeley warned of rising divorce as a by-product of an American individualism evolving into virulent egoism, "wherein the Sovereignty of the Individual—that is the right of every man to do pretty nearly as he pleases . . . is visibly gaining ground daily."[26]

As individualism intensifies, the balance of commitment can tilt so far toward the self that the family and other building blocks of society de-compose. When individualism turns into rampant wilding, as among the Ik, the family is shredded, leaving atomized individuals to prey upon one another. As the line between individualism and wilding blurs, the Amer-ican family suffers its own form of abandonment, strained to the break-ing point not only by acute economic pressures but also by the burden of its members' self-preoccupation. Americans converted to the reigning ideology of "looking out for number one" are proving ready to sacrifice not only outsiders but also their kin on the altar of their own needs and pleasures. Divorce court judge Edward M. Ginsburg concludes that the people passing through his courtroom are so committed to putting their own happiness first that it sometimes reminds him of Rome "just before it all came undone." Ginsburg muses that the role of the family has changed from caring for children to being "eternally in love and having a good time."[27]

Abandonment is a thread common to divorce and broken households. Both reflect choices to preserve the self and enhance personal happiness at the expense of the family unit, a choice that may be entirely rational when no children are involved but frequently proves catastrophic when they are. L. J. Weitzman, in her study of the children of the divorced, finds that they tend to feel abandoned, often traumatically so. They, indeed, are an abandoned population, if only because divorce is typically "financially a severe blow" for children, who lose the full economic as well as emotional support of two parents. Disruptions such as sale of the family home "adds to the trauma of children," Laurence Stone notes, "who may find themselves suddenly deprived not only of their father but also of their home, their school, their friends, and their economic comforts." Summarizing research findings, *Newsweek* concludes that "divorce has left a devastated generation in its wake."[28]

Within the two-parent household, the larger wilding culture may be leading to a more invisible emotional sabotage of the family and abandonment of children. *Newsweek* opened its special issue on the family with a critique of affluent professionals who prize their careers or BMWs more than their children. The fact that many upper-middle-class young people are taking longer to get college degrees, are flitting across careers, and are waiting longer before getting married and less time before getting divorced suggests that they find it increasingly difficult to make any commitments. This may reflect aborted emotional relations with professional parents too consumed by their own career drives to invest time in their children, who get expensive stereos and cars instead of love. Although most of these children expect to get married and have children of their own, many find the prospect frightening.

Summarizing research findings, Kenneth L. Woodward maintains that these children appear to constitute a generation that has "grown accustomed to keeping their options open. There are so many choices to make—in relationships, careers, and consumer goods—that they hate to limit their freedom." Many of these young people, beginning to suffer from their inability to make commitments, are flocking to codependency groups, a rapidly proliferating self-help movement focusing on the emotional devastation wreaked in dysfunctional families, a condition now said to include as many as 90 percent of American families.[29]

Dr. Benjamin Spock, America's best-known "family doctor," sees a direct connection between the undoing of the family and the values of our era. "By far the most disturbing force in America today," Spock says, "is excessive competitiveness. It keeps people obsessed with their jobs and with personal advancement" at the expense of feelings for others. Spock argues that the effects on the family are devastating, because it destroys the ethos of kindness and care upon which loving families depend. Spock has put his finger on the essential wilding drama of the current era: Unmitigated self-interest inevitably means abandonment of any form of family and, ultimately, as among the Ik, all social commitments.[30]

Falling Bridges, Potholes, and Peeling Schoolroom Paint: The Abandonment of Society

Journalist Tom Ashbrook, returning from a long trip to Asia, records his initial impressions. "Hello Occident. Cracked highways, no service. Hotel is heavy on glitter and self-promotional hype, light on everything else. Construction quality shabby. Rusting metalwork. Cheap materials. . . . Rich next to poor. Slick by shabby. Twitchy bag ladies and a legless panhandler croaking 'Aloha.' . . . Korean cabdriver complains road repairs take ten times longer than in Seoul."[31]

"An American homecoming," Ashbrook groans, "is a journey into shades of disarray." It is downright "scary for a recent returnee." Ashbrook, who is returning from a 10-year sojourn in Asia, learns that his brother-in-law "sleeps with a large pistol in his nightstand and an alarm system that can track a burglar room by room." Turning on the radio, Ashbrook hears of "Los Angeles drivers taking potshots at one another on the freeway, American schoolchildren scoring at the bottom of the First-World heap in key subjects. Drug lords reigning over urban fiefs, Alcoholics Anonymous and its ilk as a new religion. Wall Street sapping the economy." Fresh into his hotel, Ashbrook's son flicks on a Saturday morning cartoon: "Hey, fella! This is America," booms the wisecracking voice of an animated hero. "I've got the right to not work any time I want."[32]

"Our cracked highways and rusting bridges," writes Ashbrook, "seem physical reflections of falling standards, organization, simple care in the performance of jobs—of lost resolve." Ashbrook concludes that a "returning American comes home with trepidation," hoping that his or her sense of the breakdown of America "is exaggerated, fearing that it might not be, subtly prepared to accept it as fact."[33]

Ashbrook is seeing the unmistakable signs of a looming breakdown in both the physical and social infrastructure necessary to keep a society viable. America's physical infrastructure—its grid of roads, bridges, railways, ports, airports, sewer systems, and communications nodes—is in serious disrepair. This is no surprise to the folks in Covington, Tennessee, where a bridge over the Hatchie River collapsed, sending 7 motorists to their deaths; nor to people in upstate New York, where the collapse of a bridge killed 10 people. Nearly half of the 29,000 bridges in Massachusetts are officially "substandard." Two-thirds of these are so badly broken-down that they need to be replaced. Moreover, 70 percent of Massachusetts roads are rated "fair" or "poor." Almost everywhere "the nation's roads are crumbling . . . existing highways go unrepaired while new ones seldom advance beyond the blueprint stage. Forty percent of the nation's bridges have serious deficiencies. Airports, like highways, are strained beyond capacity, while potential mass transit options go unexplored. Water delivery systems are so antiquated that some cities still transport water through nineteenth-century wooden pipes." California Democratic congressman Robert T. Matsui says, "The problem is absolutely catastrophic"—perhaps an understatement given the price tag of repair estimated at more than $3 trillion, which is three times the size of the annual federal budget and more than the entire national debt. Rebuilding the national infrastructure, Massachusetts transportation secretary Frederick P. Salvucci says, "is the greatest public works challenge since the pyramids were built."[34]

As the physical infrastructure erodes, the social infrastructure is being quietly starved, creating an emergency in the provision of affordable housing, jobs at a livable wage, basic health care, education, and the social services required to sustain the social fabric. The crisis of affordable housing has now yielded "over three million homeless people," writes journalist Michael Albert, "who wander our backstreets eating out of garbage cans and sleeping under tattered newspapers in bedrooms shared with alley-rats." About 13 percent of Americans have fallen through the slashed social safety net and are poor, partly reflecting the unpleasant reality of an economy churning out a high proportion of extremely low wage jobs. More than 45 million Americans have no health insurance. This includes one-fifth of all American children, contributing to America's life expectancy being lower and the infant mortality rate higher than in all Western European countries and some Eastern European ones as well. Meanwhile, the collapse of American public education is yielding an average American high school student who not only has difficulty locating France, Israel, or the United States itself on a map, but scores lower across the board than students in virtually all the other advanced industrialized countries. This is well understood by American parents, who shun the public school system when they can afford to do so. An estimated 9 out of 10 Boston parents send their children to parochial school or any place other than a Boston public school.[35]

Parents recognize that American public schools are literally disintegrating. A 1995 report by the General Accounting Office showed that 25,000 U.S. schools housing 14 million children need extensive physical rehabilitation, including New York City schools with exposed asbestos, rotting roof beams, and broken plumbing; Montana schools where water leaks

have led to collapsed ceilings; and a New Orleans school where termites have eaten books on library shelves and then the shelves themselves.[36]

This abject unraveling of the social fabric is the ultimate manifestation of the new wilding culture, an abandonment of society consciously engineered by the country's political leadership and passively endorsed by the majority of voters. The cost of maintaining and reconstructing its physical and social infrastructure is well within the reach of the world's still-richest country; however, in what may be the greatest act of domestic-policy wilding in this century, recent presidents, while continuing to pour billions into the Pentagon's coffers, have refused to support the public spending that would halt and reverse the crumbling infrastructure. This refusal is rationalized under the umbrella of "free-market" ideology, to wit: rolling back taxes, deficits, and "big government." In contrast, Western European countries such as Belgium, France, West Germany, and the Netherlands, less wealthy than the United States, have managed to preserve much of their social infrastructure by spending a substantially higher percentage of their gross national product on health care, education, and a wide range of other social programs.[37]

The End of Government? Compassionate Conservatives, New Democrats, and Political Wilding

George W. Bush campaigned as a "compassionate conservative" who would "leave no child behind." While the rhetoric is appealing, the reality behind the words is less palatable. About one in every five children in America is poor, and it will take billions in education and social services to help get them out of poverty. But by making a huge $1.6-trillion tax cut the center of this presidency, Bush has undercut the children. His tax cuts will require, as we see shortly, taking money from the poor and middle class and recycling it to the rich. Moreover, as the president himself acknowledged in an address on February 18, 2001, social spending by most federal departments will have to be slashed to make the tax cuts possible, meaning that social programs for the needy will be sliced to return huge sums to the wealthy.

Massive tax-cutting has become a prime and enduring symbol of the new public-policy wilding. Cynically fueled by politicians from both parties

(Democrats in 2001 advocated a "modest" tax cut of almost $1 trillion), the so-called tax revolt has created the political space leaders need to defund society and reflects the war in Americans' hearts and minds between their commitments to society and to themselves. Cutting taxes has become the respectable political vehicle for lashing out at the poor and ultimately abandoning both government and society itself. Future historians may come to view American leaders playing the tax revolt as a sequel to Nero playing his fiddle as Rome burned.

As described shortly, tax cuts are the centerpiece of George W. Bush's presidency, with Bush seeking to complete the revolution inaugurated by Ronald Reagan. Tax cuts were at the heart of the 1980s Reagan revolution, and Reagan defined himself as a warrior against "big government." Newt Gingrich and his Republican colleagues who took over Congress in 1995, following in Reagan's footsteps, put tax-cutting at the center of their Contract With America and proposed drastically cutting nearly all social spending—from education to health care to welfare.

The Contract's tax and spending cuts were part of a systematic plan to dismantle much of the federal government itself, that is, nearly everything but military and police functions as well as the corporate welfare policies that provide subsidies for the rich and sustain corporate profitability. Gingrich described this as part of the historic Third Wave revolution, conceived by futurists Alvin and Heidi Toffler, that would sweep away central government and "devolve" power and resources to state or local governments. Despite the faddishness of the Tofflerian perspective and the dangers of "states' rights movements," which have historically helped preserve segregation and intolerance, Gingrich translated Third Wave "devolution" into a recipe for "zeroing out" a remarkable array of the most socially protective parts of the government. Among the hundreds of agencies targeted for extinction or zero public funding were the Department of Education, the National Public Broadcasting Service, the Department of Housing and Urban Development, the National Endowment for the Humanities, the National Endowment for the Arts, much of the Environmental Protection Agency, and the Federal Drug Administration.

Although in his 1995 State of the Union address President Clinton repeated his rhetorical commitment to a "new covenant" for social reconstruction, in practice he rushed to join the Tofflerian and tax revolutions, entering into competition with Republicans to see who could cut taxes and government faster. Not only did he propose his own multibillion-dollar tax cuts, targeted largely to the educated middle class rather than the rich or poor, but he also sponsored, in the name of "reinventing government," an unprecedented Democratic war on government itself. Among the agencies that the Clinton administration proposed to eliminate, privatize, or radically shrink were the Federal Aviation Administration, the Department of Transportation, the Interstate Commerce Commission, the Department of Energy, the Department of Housing, the General Services Administration, and the Office of Personnel Management. One hundred and thirty programs, including many for education, scientific research, environmental protection, and welfare, would be terminated. As one Washington observer noted: "You expect to see Republicans, when they are in power, do this—it's what they've been pushing for years. But to see Democrats doing it, and to see the competition between the White House and the Congress as they race to privatize—it's amazing."[38]

Clinton declared his own presidency the "end of big government." He showed he was serious by "ending welfare as we know it." The end of the welfare system, while celebrated in an era of hostility to government and the poor, has thrown millions of people into poverty. Although many former welfare recipients found jobs, most of the jobs do not pay enough to live on. If Clinton had replaced welfare with new programs to support working mothers with child care, affordable housing, health insurance, and a living wage, his policy might have succeeded. But by signing on to the war on government, he was not able to get Congress to fund new social safety nets.

George W. Bush has picked up where his predecessors left off, disguising his political wilding under the new rubric of compassion. He acknowledges, indeed boasts, that his proposed $1.6-trillion tax cut is the core mission of his presidency and is an attack on the welfare state. But he argues that by downsizing government, through the vehicle of tax-cutting, all will benefit, including the poor. His tax program, indeed, cuts everyone's taxes, and Bush insists this will give all Americans more control over money that is deservedly their own.

The problem is that most of the billions being returned to the people will go to the very rich. Under the Bush plan, the poorest 20 percent of the population in 2002 would receive an average tax cut of $15. The middle 20 percent would get an average cut of $170. The cut for the top 1 percent would average $13,469. As for whether Bush's overall tax-cut plan offers compassion for the ordinary worker, secretary Luwaunna Adams, a Pennsylvania mother who makes $20,400 a year, will get a tax benefit of $117 a year, or $2 a week. She appeared in a press conference with New Jersey millionaire senator Jon Corzine, who said he would get an annual tax benefit from Bush's plan of $1 million.[39]

The Democrats illustrated this huge gift to the rich when Democratic leaders Richard Gephardt, House minority leader, and Tom Daschle, Senate minority leader, appeared on Capitol Hill with a black Lexus sedan and an old, beat-up replacement muffler. Senator Daschle said that the car "was just like the Bush tax cut—fully loaded. If you're a millionaire, under the

Bush tax cut, you get a $46,000 tax cut, more than enough to pay for this Lexus. But if you're a typical working person, you get $227, and that's enough to buy this muffler."[40]

The wilding dimension of the tax cut has been highlighted, ironically, by outspoken opposition to Bush's plan from some of the world's most famous billionaires. Warren Buffet, the nation's fourth-richest person, George Soros, the world's premier global investor, and William H. Gates Sr., head of the Gates Foundation and father of Bill Gates, joined dozens of other super-rich individuals attacking the Bush plan. They zeroed in on Bush's proposal to repeal the estate, or "death," tax. Gates Sr. says that "repealing the estate tax would enrich the heirs of America's millionaires and billionaires while hurting families who struggle to make ends meet." Buffet said Bush's plan "would be a terrible mistake," the same as "choosing the 2020 Olympic team by picking the eldest sons of the gold-medal winners in the 2000 Olympics. . . . Without the estate tax," the billionaire Buffet concluded, "you in effect will have an aristocracy of wealth, which means you pass down the ability to command the resources of the nation based on heredity rather than merit."[41]

In fact, only 2 percent of the richest Americans pay the estate tax and thus would receive all the benefits of the repeal. Bush's own new head of faith-based giving, John J. DiIulio, Jr., has himself opposed repeal, since he agrees that the net effect would be to undermine the tax's financial incentive for charitable giving.[42]

It is interesting that in the one area in which Bush appears to have a genuine interest—improving education—he has proposed a modest increase in federal funding. Where the compassion is real, he retreats from his general hostility to public social spending. But even in education, the increase he proposes is, by virtually every expert account, so small that it will have little effect. While papered over by softer rhetoric, Bush's hostility to government is very clear in the details of his budget.

Making government the enemy has dangerous consequences. The right-wing terrorists who blew up the Alfred P. Murrah Federal Building in Oklahoma City on April 19, 1995, were influenced by a quarter-century of relentless attacks on government by politicians such as Ronald Reagan, Newt Gingrich, and Pat Robertson; talk-show radio personalities such as Rush Limbaugh; and the militant antigovernment ideologues who led the "patriot militias" of the 1990s. Convicted Oklahoma bomber Timothy J. McVeigh was not an isolated psychopath but a devoted disciple of extreme right wing militia movements, which have caught fire from Montana to Massachusetts. Such militias teach not only hatred of Jews, blacks, and immigrants, but a perverted individualism that sees driver's licenses, public schools, and Social Security cards as extreme infringements on personal freedom. They preach that government is the ultimate enemy of the people and should be demolished through bombings or other acts of sabotage of government installations. Militia militants, like McVeigh himself, are the bastard stepchildren of the conservative free-market fundamentalism that captured much of the nation in the 1980s and mid-1990s, and horrific wilding such as the Oklahoma City bombing will continue until the nation repudiates the antigovernment ideology that is the hallmark of the present era. Tax-cutting can serve the public interest only if it preserves the social infrastructure and protects the poor and middle class, who in the current tax revolution are paying more to support new business depreciation, capital gains, and offshore tax credits for the rich. As for government downsizing, the *New York Times*, noting that only 1 percent of the federal budget goes to welfare for the poor, proposes that human lives and much more money can be saved by slashing corporate welfare, including the billions of dollars now subsidizing agribusiness, oil, and mining industries and the billions more lost in outrageous business tax loopholes.

Jill Lancelot and Ralph De Genero suggest a "green scissors" approach to both tax-cutting and government pruning that would eliminate tax credits for companies and government programs that are ruining the environment at public expense. For starters, they suggest ending costly giveaway programs to the big mining corporations, such as the 1995 deal in which the Chevron and Manville corporations sought to pay $10,000 for national forest land in Montana estimated to be worth $4 billion in platinum deposits. To add insult to injury, such publicly subsidized mining deals lead to massive pollution, which ends up costing taxpayers an estimated $30 billion more to clean up.[43]

The assault on government is an intimate, perhaps suicidal, wilding dance between leaders and voters. Politicians and business conservatives are orchestrating the dance, according to Robert Kuttner, "channeling the raucous popular energy of the tax revolt into an orderly drive for systematic limitations on the welfare state and reductions in taxes on the well-to-do." The rich are using legitimate grievances by overtaxed homeowners and working people to reduce their own obligation to society. This proved to be such a fortuitous political recipe for the affluent that it has become the bible of the Republican party; however, what has proved to be a guaranteed ticket to elected office may prove disastrous to society as a whole, for it is doubtful that a society can survive when those governing it become accessories to its breakdown.[44]

Ordinary voters are, at minimum, being willingly seduced to dance. John Powers argues that "cafeteria-style government is on the rise in Massachusetts as more taxpayers believe that they need pay only for what they order. Yes for plowing, no for schools. Hold the bridge repairs." Powers believes that Massachusetts voters may be breaking faith with their constitution, defined as "[a] social compact, by which the whole people covenants with each Citizen and each Citizen with the whole people." In the tax revolt each voter is for himself or herself. Elderly and childless couples vote against raising taxes for schools. The young seek to ration health care for the elderly. And the well-to-do are prepared to cut back social services for the poor because in their eyes such programs are wasteful and create dependency. "Whatever happened," Powers asks, "to the common good?"[45]

Suzanne Gordon, an Arlington, Massachusetts, writer watching her neighbors acquiesce in the closing of one junior high school and two branch libraries, as well as the cutback of 30 percent of the city's workforce, sees the emergence of the "No Cares Cohort"—a "vast group of professionals between the ages of about twenty-five and forty. A lot of them don't have children till they're older, so they don't have to worry about taking care of them. They're young and healthy, so the disastrous decline in our health care system doesn't affect them. If they're married or living with someone, they're probably co-workaholics. . . . They are as removed from the social contract as those minority kids the system has truly abandoned." Gordon concludes that "our town is crumbling" because these residents are content to "sit idly by," with many "sucked into a swirl of antigovernment, antihuman frenzy. . . . The spirit of generosity seems to have been executed in Massachusetts, if not in the nation as a whole."[46]

Yet substantial majorities of taxpayers continue to tell pollsters they support earmarked spending for public universities, universal health care, and other specifically targeted social services, even as they vote against general tax increases, suggesting caution in proposing that voters have turned wholesale into mean-spirited Scrooges. Many voters say that they want to continue to help those truly in need but see government programs as a gigantic hoax and a waste, subsidizing bureaucrats rather than the poor. The public response is as much an attempt to deliver a swift kick to an overfed public bureaucracy as it is an abandonment of the needy.

My own interviews with about 30 Massachusetts voters suggest that suburbanites, affluent and geographically insulated from city life, most clearly fit the "mean-spirited" image. Many seem prepared to see the cities abandoned if their own comfortable lives could be preserved. The wilding ethos of the suburbs and the more affluent urban neighborhoods expresses itself less as a frenzied, "antihuman" rage than as an increasingly thick wall that makes the suffering of others emotionally tolerable. Most of the voters I interviewed believe that the larger society may be in danger of falling apart but find, nonetheless, a remarkable capacity to enjoy their own lives.

That a growing segment of the population is hell-bent on having a good time even as they recognize that the ship may be sinking is one of the most telling marks of the new wilding culture.[47]

Texan Justice: State Violence, Political Wilding, and the Prison–Industrial Complex

Presidents from Ronald Reagan to George W. Bush who have spearheaded the revolution against government are not telling you the truth. They do not really want to eliminate government because the capitalist economy and, especially, the superprofits of large corporations themselves depend on big government. When Ralph Nader ran for president in 2000, one of his main aims was to blast "corporate welfare"—the vast giveaways and subsidies doled out to big business. Without such help from "big government," corporate profits would rapidly decline.

The rich also need government to provide the police, prisons, and military security that protect them from the left-behinds both at home and abroad. As elites increase corporate welfare and use "trickle-up" tax policy to redistribute money to themselves, government leaders depend ever more on the use of force to contain the unrest of millions who languish in poverty, get downsized, and accumulate credit-card debt that threatens their ability to live the American Dream. In this section, we see that the massive increase in police and prisons reflects the effort to hold together by force a society that is deeply fractured by race and class.

State violence is political wilding when it involves the use of governmental force—for power or money—that ends up harming innocent people. State crime and violence have become a hot political topic in the new century. Nations around the world now seek to hold leaders accountable for war crimes, such as Serbia's deposed dictator, Slobodan Milosevic, who may be forced to appear before the International Court of Justice for genocidal campaigns of "ethnic cleansing." CIA coups against democratically elected foreign leaders, such as the one in 1973 that deposed Chile's president Salvador Allende, are another very important form of state violence that goes unpunished but constitutes egregious political wilding.[48]

The main concern here, though, is wilding practiced by our government at home. One prominent form is police brutality, symbolized most famously by the beating of Rodney King, an African-American, that triggered the Los Angeles riots in the early 1990s. The tape of the King beating, replayed on television sets across the country, showed police officers hammering King 61 times in 87 seconds with metal batons, then continuing to kick and hit him as he lay face down and motionless on the ground. Struck initially by two police Taser darts carrying 50,000 volts of electricity each, King suffered a broken leg and several broken bones in his face.

Police brutality is just one expression of an epidemic of U.S. government violence against its own citizens, especially the poor, minorities, and immigrants. Sociologist Max Weber wrote that the state can be defined as the institution vested with a monopoly of the tools of official violence, including the military, police, courts, and prisons. When governments resort to police and prisons to repress racial minorities or disadvantaged groups—or to inflict excessively harsh force against any citizens (as in the famous Waco, Texas, tragedy)—they commit political wilding.

The movement of George W. Bush from the Texas governorship to the U.S. presidency has focused attention on the huge expansion of and violence in the prison system in the last decade. When Bush was governor, Texas built more prisons and executed more people than any other state. "Texan justice" is seen by many as an oxymoron, since so many of the Texans locked up and killed are African-Americans—and so much cruelty and capriciousness is built into the system.

As governor, Bush approved the execution of Karla Faye Tucker, a confessed murderer who had undergone a deep religious conversion and been a model prisoner for two decades. Supported by thousands of religious and other civic leaders, Tucker, a national symptom of redemption and humility, sought Bush's pardon. As was reported by Tucker Carlson, a conservative journalist, for the debut of *Talk* magazine in 1999, Bush mocked Karla Faye's request for pardon by making a face and imitating her alleged despondency.

During the presidential debates, a spectator asked Bush if he was proud of all the executions he oversaw, and Bush said no. But many were looking for a more thoughtful response. The death penalty is outlawed in every European nation, and many Europeans' first reaction to Bush's election involved commentary about the barbarism of state execution and shock at Bush as a symbol of American cruelty.

In 2000, after a prisoner sentenced to death was proved innocent by DNA tests, the Republican governor of Illinois, George Ryan, suspended all executions in his state. His bold action catalyzed similar decisions in other states, where public opinion has begun to turn against the death penalty as immoral, a position long held by the Catholic Church. Whether the death penalty itself constitutes political wilding can be debated. But most agree that sentencing to death potentially innocent people who lack the money for fair legal representation and who have not been proved guilty by DNA testing and other multiple checks is unjust state violence. Moreover, experts on Texas courts and prisons have generally concluded that these flaws are blatantly evident in the Texas system and in many of the executions supervised by Bush when he was governor.

The death penalty controversy is only the tip of a rapidly escalating crisis of the prison system. More than 2 million people in 2000 were locked up in U.S. prisons, the most of any nation in the world and eight times the number incarcerated in 1970. Of these 2 million, 70 percent are minorities and half are African Americans. One of every 8 black males between the ages of 18 and 24 is in jail. "A black man in the state of California," University of California professor Angela Davis tells us, "is five times more likely to be found in a prison cell than in one of the state colleges or universities."[49]

America can barely build prisons fast enough to meet the demand. Corporations have leapt into the breach, building and operating hundreds of new prisons in the fastest-growing industry in America. Critics such as Davis have begun talking about the new "prison–industrial system." The term connotes a new melding of economic and political wilding, in which racism and poverty help fuel the growth of a huge disadvantaged prison population and the attendant prison system that returns billions of dollars in profit to wealthy investors.[50]

The new, raging controversy about "racial profiling," whereby police target minorities for random drug checks, shows that wilding begins in the prison "recruitment" process. While African-Americans consume 13 percent of illegal drugs, they comprise 74 percent of the drug offenders sentenced to prison. This reflects not only racial profiling but also massive disparities in sentences for crack compared to powder cocaine, as well as police department drug-busting on urban streets rather than suburban lots. For most offenses, minorities are disproportionately likely to be arrested, sentenced, and then physically abused by guards or denied medical treatment in jail.[51]

The prison–industrial system is not only racist but also class-biased, deeply punitive to the poor. White-collar and corporate criminals, as noted in the last chapter, steal billions more than street burglars. Yet the percentage of corporate criminals who go to jail is far lower. The prison–industrial system returns fat profits to corporate criminals who should be incarcerated in the jails that make some of them rich. Much of the profit is extracted from prisoners forced to work for wages as low as 10 cents an hour.[52]

Wilding continues upon exit from the system, since many states deny released felons the right to vote and some illegally deny the franchise even to those convicted of misdemeanors. Fourteen percent of African-American men in the United States have lost their right to vote for alleged criminal offenses, and in some states the percentage is much higher. One-third of all black men in Alabama are disenfranchised, evoking memories of Jim Crow days and the slave South.[53]

The tortured Florida election count in 2000 puts a new light on these data. As Derrick Jackson writes, "In Florida, where Al Gore lost by 537 votes, 31 percent of African-American men, 200,000 of them, cannot vote because of felony convictions. For the Florida Republican Party, that was not enough. They hired a firm to purge the rolls even more, wrongly slashing thousands of people who were guilty only of misdemeanors."[54]

The 2000 Presidential election, especially as played out in the Florida recount farce, is a case of one form of political wilding multiplied by another. At the very peak of the U.S. internal security system—which includes the judiciary as well as the prison–industrial complex—sits the Supreme Court. Bush ultimately became president because five members of the Supreme Court ruled that the Florida recount could not continue. Dissenters on the Court and hundreds of law professors have decried the decision as a historic stain on the entire judicial system.

The slim Supreme Court majority ruled that variation in counting methods in different Florida counties constituted a violation of the Fourteenth Amendment's equal-protection clause, originally passed, ironically, to protect the citizenship rights of freed slaves. But former Los Angeles deputy district attorney Vincent Bugliosi notes that "varying voting methods have been in use for two centuries; the Court has never hinted there might be a right that was being violated." Bugliosi's conclusion is stark. "These five justices," he writes, referring to the bare majority who ruled for Bush, "are criminals in every true sense of the word, and in a fair and just world belong behind prison bars." Even if one rejects Bugliosi's conclusion, there is the undeniable hint that judicial partisanship among the nation's highest judges subverted the will of the American people in electing a president. It is hard to imagine a more serious and frightening form of political wilding.[55]

Notes

1. "Boy Accused of Needle Attack." 2001. *New York Times,* February 2, p. A2.
2. Wolf, Craig. 1989. "Ten Teen-Age Girls Held in Upper Broadway Pinprick Attacks." *New York Times,* November 4, p. 27.

3. Stepp, Laura. 2000. "U.S. Survey Focuses on At-Risk Teens." 2000. *Boston Globe*, November 30, p. A4.

4. "First Grader Shot Dead at School." February 29, 2000. Retrieved 2/2001 from http://abcnews.go.com/sections/us/DailyNews/shooting000229. html.

5. "Violence in U. S. Schools." 2000. Retrieved 2/2001 from http://abc-news.go.com/sections/us/DailyNews/schoolshootings990420.html.

6. "Fears Rise of a City Consumed by Violence." 1990. *Boston Globe*, March 15, p. 12.

7. Ibid.; Jacobs, Sally. 1990. "As Streets Turn Deadly, Youths Revise Their Survival Code." *Boston Globe*, February 24, p. 1.

8. Vaishnav, Anand. 2001. "Perception and Reality in Boston's Safe Schools." *Boston Globe*, February 18, p. D3; Tippit, Sarah. 2001. "Poll Says Violence Is Common in Schools." *Boston Globe*, April 2, p. A-8.

9. Purdum, Todd S. 2001. "15-Year-Old Boy Arrested in California—Acquaintances Say He Made Threats." *New York Times*, March 6, pp. A1, A18.

10. Janofsky, Michael. 1994. "A Youth's Fatal Beating Sends Ripples through Philadelphia." *New York Times*, December 5, p. A16.

11. Matchan, Linda. 1991. "Suburban Strife." *Boston Globe*, October 28, pp. 1, 6.

12. Jones, Charisse. 1994. "An Act of Youthful Savagery Stuns a Suburb." *New York Times*, November 19, p. A1.

13. Sengupta, Somini. 2001. "Arrests Made in Darmouth Killings, but Mystery Thickens." *New York Times*, February 20, p. A12.

14. "Friendliness May Have Been Ruse for Burglaries in Small Town." 1994. *New York Times*, December 25, p. A21.

15. Johnson, Dirk. 1990. "In U.S. Parks, Some Seek Retreat, but Find Crime." *New York Times*, August 21, pp. A1, A20.

16. Ibid.

17. Ibid.

18. Turnbull, Colin. *The Mountain People.* 1987. New York: Simon & Schuster, pp. 133–34, 136.

19. Black, Chris. 1990. "The High Cost of a Gimme-Gimme Culture." *Boston Globe*, August 26, pp. A15–16.

20. Gelles, Richard J. and Murray A. Strauss. 1988. *Intimate Violence*. New York: Simon & Schuster, p. 18.

21. "Poll: 1 in 4 Jailed Killers Was Friend, Kin of Victim." 1990. *Boston Globe*, July 30, p. 5; Stacey, William and Anson Shupe. 1983. *The Family Secret*. Boston: Beacon Press, pp. 2–3, 31, 66; Bronner, Ethan. 1990. "For Youths, Family More a Threat than Strangers." *Boston Globe*, May 3, p. 1; Rosenblatt, Robert A. 1990. "Abuse of the Elderly, Most Often in Family, Is Soaring, Panel Says." *Boston Globe*, May 1, p. 10.

22. Moynihan, Daniel Patrick. 1989. "Toward a Post-Industrial Social Policy." *The Public Interest,* Fall; Stone, Lawrence. 1989. "The Road to Polygamy." *New York Review of Books,* March 2, p. 14.

23. Wetzel, James R. 1990. "American Families: 75 Years of Change." *Monthly Labor Review,* March, pp. 4–5, 9; French, Desiree. 1989. "Second Marriages." *Boston Globe,* September 19, pp. 61–62; Stone, "The Road to Polygamy," pp. 12–15.

24. Wetzel, "American Families," p. 9; Exter, Thomas. 1990. "Look Ma, No Spouse." *American Demographics,* March, p. 83. See also Sorrentino, Constance. 1990. "The Changing Family in International Perspective." *Monthly Labor Review,* March, p. 50.

25. Wetzel, "American Families," p. 11.

26. Stone, "The Road to Polygamy," p. 15.

27. Ginsburg, Edward. May 22, 1991. Cited in Barbara Carton, "Divorce: What the Judge Sees," *Boston Globe,* pp. 79, 81.

28. Weitzman, L. J. 1985. *The Divorce Reputation.* Glencoe, IL: Free Press, 1985. Stone, "Road to Polygamy," p. 14. Footlick, Jerrold. 1989. "What Happened to the Family?" *Newsweek* Special Issue on the Family, p. 16.

29. Woodward, Kenneth L. 1989. "Young Beyond Their Years," *Newsweek* Special Issue on the Family, p. 57.

30. Spock, Dr. Benjamin. 1989. "It's All Up to Us," *Newsweek* Special Issue on the Family, p. 106.

31. Ashbrook, Tom. 1989. "A View From the East," *Boston Globe Sunday Magazine,* February 19, p. 71.

32. Ibid., pp. 71–72.

33. Ibid., p. 76.

34. Mitchell, Philip. 1990. "Saving State Roads." *Boston Globe,* March, p. 11; "Aging Roads, Bridges, Get Scant Notice." 1990. *Boston Globe,* April 11, p. 20.

35. Albert, Michael. 1990. "At the Breaking Point?" *Z Magazine,* May, p. 17; DeMarco, Susan and Jim Hightower. 1988. "You've Got to Spread It Around." *Mother Jones,* May, p. 36; Sege, Irene. 1990. "Poverty, Disease, Poor Education Imperil Nation's Youth, Panel Says." *Boston Globe,* April 27, p. 6.

36. Honan, William. 1995. "14 Million Pupils in Unsuitable or Unsafe Schools, Report Says." *New York Times,* February 1, p. A21.

37. "Consensus Fuels Ascent of Europe." 1990. *Boston Globe,* May 13, p. 19.

38. Kelly, Michael. 1995. "Rip It Up." *New Yorker,* January 23, pp. 32–39.

39. Mitchell, Alison. 2001. "Moderate Republicans Oppose Bush Tax Plan as Democrats Offer Their Own." *New York Times,* February 16, p. A13.

40. "Bush Tax Plan Sent to Congress." 2001. *New York Times,* February 9, pp. A1, A14.

41. Johnston, David Cay. 2001. "Dozens of Rich Americans Join in Fight to Retain the Estate Tax." 2001. *New York Times,* February 14, pp. A1, A18.
42. "A Bad Break." 2001. *Boston Globe,* editorial, February 16.
43. Lancelot, Jill and Ralph de Genero. 1995. "Green Scissors Snip $33 Billion." *New York Times,* January 31, p. A21.
44. Kuttner, Robert. 1980. *Revolt of the Haves.* New York: Simon & Schuster, p. 10.
45. Powers, John. 1990. "Whatever Happened to the Common Good?" *Boston Globe Magazine,* April 1, pp. 16–17, 38–42.
46. Gordon, Suzanne. 1990. "Our Town Crumbles as Residents Idly Sit By." *Boston Globe,* February 24, pp. A1, A22.
47. These interviews were skillfully carried out by Boston College graduate students David Croteau and Mary Murphy.
48. Ross, Jeffery Ian, ed. 2000. *Controlling State Crime.* New Brunswick, NJ: Transaction Press.
49. Barsamian, David. 2001. "Angela Davis." *The Progressive,* February, pp. 33–38.
50. Ibid.
51. Mauer, Marc and Tracy Huling. 1995. "Young Black Americans and the Criminal Justice System: Five Years Later." Internet published (www.sentencingproject.org): The Sentencing Project.
52. Barsamian, "Angela Davis."
53. Jackson, Derrick. 2001. "Superfly Scores in Harlem." *Boston Globe,* February 16, p. A19.
54. Ibid.
55. Bugliosi, Vincent. 2001. "None Dare Call It Treason." *The Nation.* February 5, pp. 11–19.

Beyond Wilding

Resurrecting Civil Society

An injury to one is the concern of all.

—Knights of Labor motto

Wilding has taken a devastating toll on America, but it has not permanently incapacitated it. Societies, like individuals, have powerful natural resistances and remarkable capacities to regenerate themselves. While Ik society was destroyed, America, always a resilient society, has far greater economic and cultural resources to revitalize itself. To succeed, however, it will have to focus all its efforts on the task, which involves shoring up the ideal of a "civil society" at its very foundations.

Civil society is the underlying antidote to the wilding virus, involving a culture of love, morality, and trust that leads people to care for one another and for the larger community. A civil society's institutions nurture civic responsibility by providing incentives for people to act not just in their own interest but for the common good. Governments must provide a supportive framework, but a robust civil society cannot be legislated. Civil society must arise from the cooperation and moral sensibilities of ordinary people who understand that their own fulfillment requires thriving communities and an intact society.

Reflections on civil society date back to Aristotle but have been revisited in modern times following the cataclysmic changes in Eastern Europe and the Soviet Union. The dictatorial governments ruling for decades in the name of communism systematically undermined civil society, crushing all independent groups or communities that resisted their rule. As the people, already suffering from preexisting ethnic and nationalist conflicts, became increasingly atomized, unable to trust either their governments or their fellow citizens, a wilding culture emerged. It remained largely invisible, held in check by the all-powerful authorities. But after 1989, with the collapse of the Berlin Wall and the government it symbolized, the wilding forces, suppressed for so many years, were now free to surface. An epidemic erupted in the form of revived anti-Semitism, with other ethnic and ultranationalist poisons spreading through the region, including the horrific "ethnic cleansing" in Bosnia and Kosovo. After the initial revolutionary euphoria had worn off, civic indifference, apathy, and a lack of trust and cooperation developed among citizens. Calls for the resurrection of civil society have reverberated from Budapest and Prague to Moscow, with some leaders, such as the Czech Republic's president Vaclav Havel, recognizing that the biggest challenge after decades of rule under the rhetoric of collectivism, is, ironically, the rebuilding of community.

The wilding crises in Eastern Europe and the United States are different from one another; one was bred by coercive collectivism and the other by untrammeled free-market individualism. Sociologist Alan Wolfe writes that both an overreaching government and an overblown market can, in different ways, colonize civil society and destroy it—the market, by glorifying selfishness, and the state, by substituting paternalism or coercion for conscience. Civil society blooms only where markets and governments are kept in reasonable check, and families, communities, and voluntary associations, the institutional seedbeds of love, morality, and trust, are free to prosper. The bonds of conscience and caring, as well as mechanisms of social accountability to be discussed below, help to ensure that private interests do not override the common good.[1]

Although there is no magic formula and no perfect model, civil society is the strongest and most suitable medicine for the wilding epidemic. Americans now urgently must recognize that they must dedicate themselves unwaveringly to reconstructing their society.

The Case for Hope

More than 150 years ago, Alexis de Tocqueville worried that America was vulnerable to an individualism that "saps the virtues of public life" and "in the long run" might "attack and destroy" society itself. Tocqueville described it as an individualism "which disposes each member of the community to sever himself from the mass of his fellows," and to "feel no longer bound by a common interest." Americans must always be on guard, Tocqueville advised, against the deterioration of their individualistic culture into "a passionate and exaggerated love of self, which leads a man to connect everything with himself, and to prefer himself to everything else in the world."[2]

Tocqueville did not disapprove of the healthy self-interest that energized Americans, but he saw the thin line separating American individualism from wilding. Without strongly developed moral codes, the restless pursuit of self-interest inherent in a market economy could at any time degrade into an egoistic menace that might destroy society. But Tocqueville, a sober observer, was also extraordinarily optimistic about the American experiment. Counteracting the wilding virus was another side of America, the strength of its civil society. One manifestation was the personal generosity and helpfulness that he observed in all his American travels. "Although private interest directs the greater part of human actions in the United States," Tocqueville wrote, "it does not regulate them all. I must say that I have often seen Americans make great and real sacrifices to the public welfare; and I have remarked a hundred instances in which they hardly ever failed to lend faithful support to each other." Because an American is neither master nor slave to his fellow creature, "his heart readily leans to the side of kindness."[3]

Tocqueville recognized that the kinder and gentler side of American life was grounded in the political rights and free institutions that "remind every citizen, and in a thousand ways, that he lives in society." Tocqueville marveled at Americans' propensity to "constantly form associations" of a thousand kinds in which they "voluntarily learn to help each other." Americans were constantly connecting and spontaneously creating the bonds of friendship, trust, and cooperation that lie at the heart of civil society.[4]

In the century and a half since Tocqueville's visit, the wilding epidemic has spread throughout America, but it has not totally destroyed the civil society that made such an impression on him. Much evidence suggests that Americans retain some of the openness, generosity, and moral idealism that, in Tocqueville's view, differentiated them from Europeans. Likewise, the free institutions and "propensity to associate" have not vanished. It is the sturdiness of this base, its survival in the face of the wilding onslaught, that offers grounds for optimism and a direction for the future.

Each year in Boston, more than 50,000 people join the Walk for Hunger. The marchers hike for 20 miles, often in inclement weather, to raise money for Project Bread, a group that helps provide meals for the homeless and hungry. Each participant takes time to approach sponsors, who agree to donate a certain amount of money for each mile that the walker completes. As one curbside viewer said, "You've got the elderly walking, you've got kids walking, you've got families walking. To me, it's the most beautiful sight to see all the people walking." Such walks are only one of a cornucopia of charitable endeavors that regularly take place in cities and towns across the United States.

At the very time that taxpayers are revolting and turning off the public spigot, volunteers are stepping in to help stop the bleeding that their own votes have precipitated. In many towns across the country, playground construction is done mainly by volunteers, in the spirit of traditional community barn-raising. In Plymouth, Massachusetts, the town library stays open only because of the generosity of more than 50 volunteers; in nearby Raynham, the school libraries are run entirely by volunteers. Community booster groups rally to raise money to keep public buildings painted, keep school sports programs going, and plant trees and maintain the city parks.[5]

Even in the heart of Wall Street there are signs of the other America. Several multimillionaire commodities traders created the Robin Hood Foundation, an offbeat center that scours New York City "looking for neighborhood foundations that rescue the homeless, care for children with AIDS, fight drug abuse, or rebuild families." The organization seeks to link community activists to business sponsors or technical experts who can be helpful. One of the founders says, "I couldn't sleep if I did not have a part in this sort of thing," and another says, "I love this city with a passion. I'm a walking poster for New York. I don't want to see the city go under."[6]

Such anecdotes are backed up by hard statistics documenting the generous side of America. About 7 out of every 10 households contribute to charity, donating an average of almost 2 percent of household income, a figure almost four times greater than that in Canada and England (a comparison that should take into account the national health plans and large social welfare programs that taxpayers in the latter countries support, thereby reducing the need for charity). About 45 percent of Americans over the age of 18 sacrifice their own time to volunteer, averaging about four hours a week and totaling almost 20 billion hours of volunteer time nationwide.[7]

How can the wilding epidemic spread at the same time that moral commitments and compassionate behavior persist at these levels? As I argued in Chapter 1, America is host simultaneously to a wilding culture and a civil culture, with sectors of the elites increasingly immersed in wilding and a vast number of ordinary Americans uneasily straddling the two cultures. Most Americans' lives are a struggle to reconcile wilding impulses with a nagging conscience that refuses to die. Many succumb to wilding pressures at the office but discover their humanity with family or friends. Conversely, some become wilders in their personal lives but express their conscience in admirable careers dedicated to constructive professional or business enterprise, public service, or social change.

The stubborn persistence of civil society and moral commitment provides a fertile seedbed for social reconstruction. The way to stop the wilding epidemic is to bolster all the empathic and moral sensibilities that

Americans already display. Although these need to be fortified and mobilized with new visions, the project is more akin to catalyzing the surviving immune system of a weakened patient than seeking to transplant a new immune system to the patient whose own defenses have been destroyed.

But solving the problem will take serious cultural and institutional change. As I have argued, wilding grows out of an American individualism that is deeply rooted. The country's leadership and major institutions increasingly fuel Americans' wilding side and provide serious disincentives to their less egoistic inclinations. We need the culture, economics, and politics of a civil society, where the rules of the success game encourage attention to morality and the common good. More precisely, we must rewrite the rules of the game such that those who neglect the collective interest will not prosper and those who take it into account will realize their just rewards.

Rethinking the American Dream: A New Communitarianism?

The American Dream has not always been a cultural template for wilding. As we consider rewriting the dream for a better future, we have the consolation that we can look to our history for guidance. Through most of America's past, the purely materialistic and individualistic side of the dream has been balanced by a moral and community-oriented side, preventing the dream from transmuting into a wilding recipe. Moreover, the dream has been inclusive, defining a set of common purposes to which all Americans could aspire. These historical features of the dream need to be recaptured in order to fortify civil society and purge the wilding epidemic.

The individualistic dream dominating today has its roots in the mythology of the self-made man and, as James Combs argues, "stems from the ideology of capitalism and the myth of unlimited abundance." The nineteenth-century novelist Horatio Alger immortalized the materialist Dream in his rags-to-riches fables. In its current form, it celebrates American heroes such as basketball superstar Michael Jordan, who rose to fabulous success through his extraordinary individual talent and hard work.[8]

The materialistic dimensions of the dream have become so dominant that most Americans have forgotten that there was once another side to the dream. America has traditionally defined itself in terms of a set of high

moral ideals, including democracy, equality, and tolerance. Values growing out of the religious and political foundations of the country, including the Puritan zeal for community and the American Revolution's ideal-
ization of civil democracy, helped to shape another dream, one that
mythologized family, community, and civic responsibility. Through most
of American history, the materialistic dream prevailed, but the dream that
elevated community values warned that success should not be achieved at
any price. America idealized its rural and small-town communities where,
to a greater or lesser degree, as Combs notes, "religion, family, and democratic good feelings tempered the quest for power and money." Small-
town community is still part of American mythology, helping explain why
President Clinton proudly publicized his roots in the town of Hope,
Arkansas, and President Bush II speaks nostalgically of his boyhood in a
tiny Texan town.[9]

The two dreams define a creative tension in American history. In the
1930s, the Great Depression mobilized Americans to rally together and
fashion a collective lifeline to ride out the economic storm. President
Franklin Delano Roosevelt reinvigorated the dream of moral community,
using the government to affirm that in a time of desperate need, Americans would take care of each other. Three decades later, in the 1960s, a
whole generation of youth plunged into social activism and communal
experiments, seeking a morally attractive alternative to the materialist
dream of their 1950s childhoods.

The failure of the aspirations of the 1960s has led, in the decades since
then, to perhaps the most extensive subordination of the moral dream in
American history. To purge the wilding epidemic, Americans in the twenty-
first century will have to rediscover and refashion a version of the moral
dream in order to temper the current fever of individualistic materialism
and resurrect civil society.

The moral vision will have to be creative because of the new threats that
unchecked materialism now poses. It will have to encompass an ecological
morality, for we now know that the untrammeled materialist dream is in-
compatible with planetary survival, becoming a form of wilding directed
against nature itself. Global warming, the catastrophic heating up of the
earth through promiscuous use of fossil fuels, is only the most frightening
of the legacies of such environmental wilding. If Americans cannot learn
to live within the limits dictated by the environment, they will be engaged
not only in crimes against nature but in a form of wilding against future
generations who will bear the ultimate consequences.

Americans find it hard to accept any limits on materialism, for the dominant dram has equated freedom and fulfillment with the right to get as
rich or famous as luck, talent, or hard work permits. To suggest that Bill

124

Gates should not have been allowed to make or keep the nearly $100 bil-
lion he now has strikes us as un-American. But a civil society must respect
not only ecological limits but also those dictated by the traditional American morality of fair play and egalitarianism. Uncapping all limits in the recent orgy of greed and deregulation has polarized the country, creating an
unprecedented and morally unbearable division between rich and poor.[10]

Civil society is a society of inclusion, and the new dream will have to
script new trade-offs between individual freedom and the survival of the
community. This ultimately requires reviving a moral dream of community; not the utopian vision of communes that failed in the 1960s, but
something simultaneously more modest and more ambitious: a reawak-
ening of the American sense of community that can mobilize the country to unify and preserve itself in an era of unprecedented division.

The Social Market:
Sociological Sense and Dollars and Cents

As Americans have struggled to choose between the materialist dream and
the moral dream, they have had to wrestle with the tensions between the
free market and community. The market system is an excellent vehicle for
delivering the promises of the materialist dream, but it is far less effective
in preserving the moral fiber of society. In periods when the moral dream
has come more strongly to the fore, such as the 1930s and 1960s, Americans have pioneered economic models, such as the New Deal and the Great
Society, that depart from free-market scripture.

Europeans have spent an entire century building an alternative with a
social conscience to the free market. The Swedes, Danes, Austrians, and
Germans recognize that they are not playing Adam Smith's game. "We are
not operating a marketplace economy," admits German industrialist Hel-
mut Giesecke, but rather a "social marketplace economy [that] guarantees
food, shelter, schooling, and medical attention to every person, not as welfare but as human rights." Government, labor, and business work together
to reconcile prosperity with social justice. German business has supported
this program, according to Giesecke, because "this social network really
works," leading to a well-educated, healthy, and motivated workforce
whose productivity keeps increasing.[11]

Perhaps ultimately the Germans support the social infrastructure because they know firsthand the horrific consequences when society totally

breaks down. They have experienced a Germany gone completely wild, and many recognize that it could happen again. The greater internal homogeneity of Germany, Austria, Sweden, and other European "social market" societies also allows them to feel a greater connection to others and to savor the sense of family. Even as European cultures grow more individualistic and consumerist, their social marketplace economies may prevent a descent into wilding.

The development of an American social market could be one of the most potent remedies for the wilding epidemic. It would provide a way to reconcile economic growth and justice, and to help solve America's social problems by building on its own deepest value: democracy.

The social market is the economic recipe for a civil society, but the Western Europe version is not the one Americans are likely to embrace. The European model is a universal welfare state, in which the government shelters groups unprotected by the market; responds to the medical, housing, and social needs of the population that the market neglects; and comprehensively regulates business to ensure social responsibility. But American history, as well as its current fiscal crisis, argues against the likelihood that Americans, barring another Great Depression, will look solely to the state; although there is a crucial role for government to play in stopping the wilding epidemic, it can only be a catalyst, not the central player.

The key to a social market system is not big government but new institutions, whether public or private, that rectify the tendency of our current market economy to write social costs and benefits out of the equation. The American free market responds mainly to the desires of the individual actor—whether a person or corporation—and is largely indifferent to the spillover effects that transactions may have on the rest of society. When a factory decides to pollute, the social cost of bad air and ensuing discomfort or respiratory disease is what economists call an externality, a real cost, but one that the factory owner can ignore, because it is society rather than the factory that pays the ultimate bill. In the pure free-market model, there is neither an economic incentive for the individual to help society nor a market disincentive to be antisocial; the market simply does not discriminate, operating with so-called benign neglect. As such neglect accumulates, with the market turning a blind eye to the millions of externalities that affect society every day, benign neglect becomes catastrophic social blindness and civil society is placed in jeopardy.

A social market corrects such social blindness by writing social costs and benefits back into the equation. It is a market that seeks to internalize the externalities, thus becoming socially responsible by giving social stakeholders a voice in corporate decisions and by devising strategies to guarantee that economic wilders will pay the cost of their sociopathic behavior (and, conversely, that the good citizen will receive his or her just rewards). One way to do this is to rely on government, which can compel prosocial choices through legislation or induce them through tax incentives, as when the state enforces worker health and safety standards or gives tax credits to factories installing antipollution devices. But there is another approach, one more appealing to Americans wary of government and committed to democracy, that involves redesigning economic institutions to be better equipped to exercise social responsibility on their own initiative. One such approach involves new corporate ownership and participation arrangements, in which workers and local citizens gain a voice and can speak up for the needs of the larger community. The Germans, although relying primarily on government, also have invented a "co-determination" system, which requires that every industrial enterprise with more than 500 workers select half its governing board of trustees from among its own employees. This has been successful for more than 40 years, contributing not only to the German economic boom but to a civil industrial society in which ordinary workers have been able to ensure that their health and safety are protected, their grievances addressed, and their jobs protected by investment strategies that prioritize domestic employment as well as overseas profit. Co-determination is a version of economic democracy that works.

Sociologist Severyn Bruyn describes the many down-to-earth ways, some already highly developed in America, to fashion a social market that works to dissuade economic wilding and preserve civil society without resorting to big government. Numerous forms of worker ownership and participation, including cooperatives and employee stock ownership plans (ESOPs), in which employees own a piece or all of their companies, can help compel the company to treat its employees fairly and practice workplace democracy. The cooperative, as its name implies, has the potential to turn the workplace itself into a civil society, because everyone within it has equal rights, and self-interest is more closely wedded to the collective interest than in a conventional firm. Another innovation involves corporate social charters that bind businesses to serve designated social missions, as in the case of community credit unions that are structured to reinvest in the community and offer low-interest loans to poorer residents. Land trusts, modern versions of the colonial concept of the commons, can remove property from the commercial market and legally ensure that it is used to serve community needs. A new field of social accounting can help take stock of the social costs and benefits of corporate decisions. Social capital, such as the trillions of dollars in American pension funds, one of the largest and still-growing pots of money in the world, can be used to invest in affordable housing and community economic development. The new practice of social investing could be the first step in turning the stock market into what sociologist Ritchie

Lowry calls "good money," where investors seek a profit but also a social return on their money. "Social screens"—report cards on companies compiled by outside analysts—now tell investors which corporations are economic wilders and which are responsible citizens. Companies seeking to attract the funds of millions of social investors have to demonstrate not only what they are doing for the bottom line but what they are doing for their communities.[12]

America has not yet built a main highway toward this version of the social market, but it is already carving out many smaller roads in that direction. There are now more than 10,000 American ESOPs, including huge companies such as United Airlines, Avis Rent-a-Car, and Weirton Steel, and there is evidence that they are more responsive to their employees and their customers. Studies show that worker-owners are more productive and deliver higher quality, with Avis now number one in ratings of customer satisfaction. Hundreds of ESOPs and cooperatives, including large worker-owned factories, practice sophisticated forms of workplace democracy. They are proving effective in job creation and retention, and are responsible for saving hundreds of jobs during the epidemic of factory closings in the last decade. According to polls, including one by Peter Hart, economic democracy makes sense to most Americans; approximately 70 percent say that they would welcome the opportunity to work in an employee-owned company.[13]

The thousand American companies with the highest percentage of employee ownership constitute the nucleus of a new social market sector of the economy. The proliferation of 401K retirement plans, in which workers receive pension benefits in the form of employee stocks, will increase the size and power of this new economic sector. If these companies sustain employee loyalty, high productivity, and robust profits, they will teach a much wider range of American companies and employees about the virtues of both employee ownership and social market values.

The political genius of social market innovations is that they are attractive to liberals, because they promote equality and justice, as well as to conservatives, because they do not require massive government intervention and do offer ordinary citizens a greater stake in the marketplace. In the 1970s, Senator Russell Long, a conservative Democrat from Louisiana, was the prime sponsor in the Senate for employee-ownership legislation, and the idea found considerable support in the Reagan White House as a strategy for building "people's capitalism." Liberal activists in universities, unions, and local communities also fight for employee ownership, as a way to save jobs and increase workers' control.

Any idea that can draw such enthusiastic support from both sides of the political spectrum has the potential to be instituted on a large scale. At the same time, however, most of the more radical social market innovations have been resisted by powerful forces, as in the case of banks systematically denying credit to cooperatives. Mainstream businesses and politicians have also worked to water down innovations such as ESOPs to keep them from turning real decision-making power over to workers. Nonetheless, those who seek real solutions to America's wilding crisis should hone the idea of the social market as a new public philosophy and the basis of a new legislative agenda.

Although government is not the prime mover in this emerging social market, it has helped midwife the new system and will have to play a much greater role if a new market order is to grow and become preservative of civil society. Government has to set up the legislative framework for corporate social charters, ESOPs, and worker cooperatives; establish the legal safeguards and guidelines for social investment of pension funds; provide encouragement through loans and tax credits for employee ownership and community-development funds; and help oversee and underwrite the entire new economic nexus. Its regulatory role will remain powerful for many years and will never disappear, for, as suggested below, many public interests can be guaranteed only by the state. The government will not give the marching orders or own the means of production as it does under communism or socialism; the social market is still a market system, infused with sensibilities of community.

There is special urgency now regarding children. One of every four American children lives in poverty, and public policy threatens to guarantee that the next generation will mature into uninhibited wilders. As civil society unravels, children are the most vulnerable group, being totally dependent on the love, moral guidance, and social spending that are casualties of the wilding culture. The state cannot raise and socialize children, but one of its highest priorities should be to help finance and save the institutions, including the family and schools, that can do the job. These are now in such desperate condition that further benign neglect is unacceptable; moreover, sensible and economical family and educational strategies have already been articulated by numerous national commissions and children's advocates such as the Children's Defense Fund. No antipoverty social market programs are utopian, and none need to be budget-busters.

The rise of the embryonic social market is part of a second American revolution, this one to ensure economic rights and to save the society liberated by the Revolution more than 200 years ago. Then, the issue was inventing a political constitution; now it involves rewriting the economic constitution. As in the first Revolution, ordinary citizens will have to struggle against powerful, entrenched forces, the King Georges of contemporary America who are more dedicated to their own privileges than to saving civil society in America.

A New Bill of Rights?
The Politics of Civil Society

America's romance with individualism and the free market has its virtues, but it has clouded Americans' understanding of what makes society tick. Civil society arises only when individuals develop strong obligations to the larger "us" that can override the perennial, very human preoccupation with the self. Such larger commitments bloom only under special conditions: when the community shows that it cares so deeply for each of its members that each, in turn, fully understands his or her debt to society and seeks to pay it back in full.

The Japanese and Europeans, in their very different ways, seem to appreciate this deal, or contract, that preserves civil society. Japanese corporations smother the Japanese worker in a cocoon of secure employment, health benefits, housing, and other social necessities that make it almost impossible for workers to imagine life outside of the group. Through their expansive welfare states, the Europeans deliver their own bushel of benefits and entitlements that the citizen recognizes as indispensable to personal survival and happiness. Both systems possess their own serious problems and are partially eroding in the face of global economic pressures, but they continue to succeed in creating the allegiance to the larger community that breeds immunity to the wilding epidemic.

Each civil society has to find its own way of inspiring its members' devotion, but all must deliver those rock-bottom necessities essential to the pursuit of life, liberty, and happiness. These include a minimal level of personal safety, food, shelter, and a livelihood. Social orphans deprived of these essentials are unable to fulfill any larger obligation to society, for their existence is entirely consumed by the brutish struggle for personal survival.

This leads to the idea of social citizenship, an extension of the familiar but narrower concept of political citizenship. The rights to health care, housing, and a job can be seen as social rights, parallel to our political rights to the franchise and to free speech enshrined in our Constitution. Political rights apply to all citizens automatically, because they are the precondition of democracy as a system. Similarly, social rights should be extended automatically to everyone, for they are the precondition of civil society's survival.

The Japanese deliver such social rights through a paternalistic, corporate, extended family, largely private, whereas the Europeans do it through the welfare state. America will have to find its own way. Ideally, the emerging institutions of the social market would, in the long run, provide a local, democratic, and nonstatist solution. One possibility is an American version of the success achieved by Mondragon, a remarkable complex of more than 100 industrial cooperatives in the Basque region of Spain. Mondragon has succeeded during the past 40 years in guaranteeing job security, housing, health care, and education to its members with scarcely any help from the state. Workers in the cooperatives have created cooperative schools, hospitals, insurance companies, and banks that offer robust social security from birth to death. The Mondragon complex, which is the largest manufacturer of durable goods in Spain and employs thousands of worker-owners, has never permanently laid off a worker, reproducing the equivalent of the Japanese system of lifetime employment, while also inventing new cooperatives in one of the most impressive programs of job creation in the world.

Whether an American social market could evolve in such a direction is purely speculative, but clearly there are ways to provide social rights that are realistic, democratic, and do not require big and overly intrusive government. America is the only major industrialized country not to offer health care as a social right to all its citizens. In Germany and other European countries, the federal government is involved in collecting taxes to support national health care but allows provincial councils and local communities to administer their own programs.

Although government is not the preferred agent, it has a leading role to play in areas such as education, health care, and social welfare, where human need rather than profit is the only acceptable moral compass. Government is also the guarantor of last resort. When people are homeless, starving, or jobless, civil society has failed, and a wilding virus is activated. It is not silly idealism or bleeding-heart liberalism, but a conservative and prudent defense of the social order that requires public action.

For this reason, legal scholars such as Columbia University law professor Louis Henkin are pointing to "genetic defects" in our Bill of Rights that constitutionally guarantee political but not social citizenship rights. Chief Justice William Rehnquist, in a 1989 Supreme Court decision, argued that the Constitution confers "no affirmative right to governmental aid, even when such aid may be necessary to secure life." This leads constitutional attorney Paul Savoy, former dean of the John F. Kennedy University School of Law, to point out that "our civil rights and civil liberties are rights in the negative sense" and "do not include affirmative obligations on government. We do not have a constitutional right to have the state provide us with health care, or give us shelter if we are homeless, or prevent a child from being beaten or from starving to death." A coalition of unions, environmentalists, and community groups have responded by calling for a second Bill of Rights that would entitle all citizens to the elementary social rights of shelter, food, and health care.

Such social rights have already been embraced by most nations of the world and by the United Nations. The 1948 UN Universal Declaration of Human Rights explicitly embraces rights of all people to employment, shelter, education, and health care. The International Labor Organization, a UN agency, spells out the rights of all workers to associate freely in unions of their choice and to earn a living wage. There are also UN agreements on the rights of women, children, and the environment. Unfortunately, many of these rights are not enforced—and the UN has no mechanism to do so. To combat wilding in the global economy, it is essential that the U.S. government, a signatory of many of the UN human rights documents, move aggressively to support international means of enforcing social rights both abroad and at home.[14]

Social rights are not a free ride for the population, for with them come demanding social obligations. Citizenship is an intimate dance of rights and obligations, and social citizens need to enthusiastically embrace the moral obligations that come with their new entitlements. This means not only willingly paying the taxes required to keep civil society healthy, but also devoting time and effort, as detailed below, to community-building at work, in the neighborhood, and in the country at large.

The problem with the Left is that it demands rights without spelling out the obligations that have to accompany them; the problem with the Right is that it expects obligations to be fulfilled without ceding social rights in return. Both positions are absurd, because rights and obligations are flip sides of civil society's coin of the realm. We need a new politics that marries the Left's moral passion for rights with the Right's sober recognition of duty.

Defending Our Lives: Getting from Here to There

But what do we do now? Americans are a pragmatic people and want down-to-earth answers. Although there is no recipe or magic formula, we can act now to stop the wilding epidemic. If we want to survive with our humanity intact, we have no alternative.

Since wilding can destroy society, we are all fighting to stay alive. Obviously, if we each felt we had a desperate illness, we would mobilize ourselves to act immediately, to save ourselves. But since wilding is a societal crisis, not a biological illness, individuals can feel a deceptive immunity.

It is possible to feel healthy, have fun, and enjoy life as society begins to come undone.

But as the epidemic spreads, everyone will increasingly feel at risk. The personal meaning of the wilding crisis is that we each have to spend more and more time simply defending our lives, defending our property, defending our livelihood, defending our health, defending our physical safety, defending our ego. This imposes a terrible burden on the individual, and it can easily fuel the "me" mentality at the heart of the problem, but it also unlocks the riddle of what to do. Not only will the illusion of immunity diminish, but the wisdom of dealing with the underlying disease, not just the symptoms, will become more apparent.

One can start defending one's life, as Albert Brooks's 1990s film comedy of that title suggests, either wisely or foolishly. The shortsighted approach involves trying to save oneself by abandoning everyone else, exemplified by the suburbanites who cocoon themselves within homes wired with the latest security technology and who refuse to pay taxes to support the center city. Robert Reich suggests that such a "politics of secession" is sweeping upper-middle-class America. If so, it is a blind and morally unsustainable choice, for it creates short-term symptomatic relief while worsening the disease.

Because the disease is social, so, too, must be the cure. As the social infrastructure begins to ulcerate and bleed, the rational long-term way to defend one's life is to help repair the damaged societal tissue, whether it be potholes in the road, hungry people sleeping on grates, or sociopathic competitiveness at the office. Doing the right thing, then, is defending one's life by cooperating to build up community strength and bolster personal and collective resistance. This requires no saintly sacrifice for the common good, but rather a tough-minded and clear-eyed assessment of where the threat lies. When facing a wilding threat, the first question to ask is, "What in myself or my social environment is creating this threat?" Once that question is answered, the next one is, "What can I do about it?" Some cases will require purely personal change, falling back on all one's psychological and moral strength, as well as love and support from family, friends, or mentors, to counter wilding impulses within oneself or susceptibility to wilding influence in the environment. Most cases will also require acting for some form of social change to extirpate the external poison, whether at work, in the neighborhood, or in the White House, typically achievable only with the help of others.

Fortunately, the wisdom of social action is obvious in a huge variety of circumstances, and Americans are already responding, especially where their own health is involved. When kids in Woburn, Massachusetts, were getting sick because of toxic chemicals, parents got together to clean up the toxic dump and hold the wilding factory accountable. Americans are recognizing that staying healthy has become a political action project requiring a massive environmental cleanup, and they are not waiting for lackadaisical governments to take the lead. "People are recognizing they can in fact control their environment," Hal Hiemstra, a Washington environmental activist notes. "They're starting to say, 'we've had it.'" The *Boston Globe* reports that "an environmental wake-up call [is] being sounded nationwide by communities alarmed by the federal government's inertia and inspired by their own sense of power to reshape the landscape." These activists are not only defending their lives but, the *Globe* observes, "are local heroes on planetary matters."[15]

Heroes of a different sort are the residents of suburban communities around Minneapolis, who swam against the tide and rejected the politics of secession, the suburban wilding that helped push Bridgeport, Connecticut, into Chapter Eleven bankruptcy and left New York City and hundreds of other cities teetering on the brink. The Minnesota suburbs joined with Minneapolis to form a regional pact "whereby any community enjoying 40 percent more than the average growth of the region in any given year would have to share with the other signers of the pact." Such apparent sacrifice for the larger good is just plain common sense, because if the city center failed, it would bring the surrounding communities down with it. The great irony, as John Shannon of the Urban Institute notes, "is that Minneapolis is now enjoying boom times and must pay out to the suburbs." A modern Aesop's fable, it shows how cooperation for the common good is, indeed, a form of enlightened self-interest.[16]

We can begin to cure the wilding sickness by doing more of what we have always done well and doing it better: taking responsibility for our lives through civic participation. Tocqueville was amazed at the richness of America's democracy; its dense web of voluntary associations and democratic town meetings made it unique. "The free institutions which the inhabitants of the United States possess, and the political rights of which they make so much use," Tocqueville explained, "remind every citizen, and in a thousand ways, that he lives in society." In other words, democracy, and more democracy, is the best antidote for wilding and the most nourishing food for the social infrastructure.[17]

Americans have become apathetic and indifferent to national politics, but we still retain our propensity to join together in what Tocqueville called "an immense assemblage of associations." One researcher suggests that there are now more than 500,000 self-help groups in the United States, with more than 15 million members; many, whether alcoholics, abused children, battered spouses, or codependents, are casualties of the wilding epidemic who, by joining with others, are taking enlightened first steps toward not only recovering personally but also rebuilding civil society. The same can be said of the millions of others involved in volunteer efforts and political activism at local or higher levels.[18]

Millions of Americans recognize that giving back can be both fun and morally compelling, and they are serving their communities in movements to help the homeless, feed the hungry, care for AIDS patients, tutor the illiterate, protect the environment, and help organize America's workers and poor people. Many recognize that in addition to individual volunteers, we need sustained social movements that can provide the voice and muscle for ordinary citizens against the power of giant, greedy corporations and unresponsive government. This will require, most of all, the resurrection of a labor movement that speaks for social justice and economic democracy.

On my own campus, many students who have engaged in community service work have begun to realize that service is not enough. While it helps individuals in trouble, it does not solve the societal problems that put them in difficulty in the first place. Students who work in soup kitchens begin to ask why there are so many hungry people, and those working in battered women's shelters ask why there is so much domestic violence. This leads them to the recognition that it will take collective action aimed at changing institutions, that is, social movements, to truly solve the underlying causes of the problems that plague the people they want to help.

Anti-sweatshop activists on campus have joined forces with the labor movement to end corporate wilding here and around the world. The labor movement, while demonized by many U.S. business leaders, is becoming a genuine voice for the community at large. Recall that "solidarity forever" has always been the rallying cry of the labor movement and that as corporations threaten community at home and abroad, the very concept of "union" tells us what we need: people coming together to defend human values against greed and exploitation.

Other social movements are also vital for people seeking to end the wilding crisis. I discussed in Chapter 4 the post-Seattle global justice movement that is bringing together students, workers, environmentalists, feminists, and civil rights groups from around the world to forge a new world community based on human rights rather than money. Each of these movements has its own agenda essential to combating aspects of the wilding crisis; as they learn to work together for justice at home and abroad, they offer the best chance to make a difference that we have seen for a long time. Anyone concerned with the wilding crisis should learn about these different movements and join up. For in these movements lies the chance not only of changing the world but of creating a new form of community for oneself.

Americans' indifference to national politics reflects less pure selfishness or apathy than despair about leaders and the absence of real choices. America desperately needs a new generation of political leaders who will tell the truth about the wilding crisis and articulate a new moral vision. But because no such leaders are now in view, the burden falls on the rest of us, where it ultimately belongs.

Notes

1. Wolfe, Alan. 1989. *Whose Keeper? Social Science and Moral Obligation.* Berkeley: University of California Press, 1989.
2. Tocqueville, Alexis de. [1840] 1985. *Democracy in America.* Vol. II. (New York: Knopf), pp. 119–20, 121, 123.
3. Ibid., p. 128.
4. Ibid., p. 129.
5. Preer, Robert. 1991. "Volunteers Plug Cash Gap in the Suburbs." *Boston Globe,* June 9, pp. 1, 8.
6. Teltsch, Kathleen. 1991. "Nowadays, Robin Hood Gets the Rich to Give to the Poor." *New York Times,* June 3, p. B1.
7. Hodgkinson, Virginia Ann and Murray S. Weitzman. 1989. *Dimensions of the Independent Sector.* Washington, DC: Independent Sector, pp. 7–9.
8. Combs, James. 1984. *Polpop: Politics and Popular Culture in America.* Bowling Green, OH: Bowling Green University Popular Press, p. 29.
9. Ibid., p. 34.
10. Phillips, Kevin. 1990. *Politics of Rich and Poor.* New York: Random House, chap. 1.
11. "Consensus Fuels Ascent of Europe." 1990. *Boston Globe,* May 13, p. 19.
12. Bruyn, Severyn. 1991. *A Future for the American Economy.* Stanford, CA: Stanford University Press. See also Bruyn, Severyn. 1987. *The Field of Social Investment.* Cambridge: Cambridge University Press; Bruyn, Severyn and James Meehan. 1985. *Beyond the Market and the State.*

Philadelphia: Temple University Press; Lowry, Ritchie. 1991. *Good Money.* New York: W. W. Norton.

13. Bruyn, *A Future for the American Economy.*

14. Savoy, Paul. 1991. "Time for a Second Bill of Rights." *The Nation,* June 17, pp. 815–16.

15. Tye, Larry. 1991. "Local Heroes on Planetary Matters." *Boston Globe,* June 22, p. 3.

16. Loth, Renee. 1991. "Small Cities, Big Problems." *Boston Globe,* June 23, pp. A25, A28.

17. Tocqueville, *Democracy in America.*

18. Marx, Gary T. 1994. "Fragmentation and Cohesion in American Society." In R. Dynes and K. Tierney, *Disasters, Collective Behavior, and Social Organization,* Newark, DE: University of Delaware Press.

Acknowledgments

137

Grateful acknowledgment is made for permission to reprint the following:

James Alan Fox and Jack Levin, excerpts from "Inside the Mind of Charles Stuart," *Boston Magazine* (April 1990). Copyright © 1990 by Boston Magazine, Inc., a subsidiary of METROCORP. Reprinted with the permission of *Boston Magazine.*

Kathleen Hughes and David Jefferson, excerpts from "Why Would Brothers Who Had Everything Murder Their Parents?" *The Wall Street Journal* (March 20, 1990). Copyright © 1990 by Dow Jones & Company, Inc. Reprinted with the permission of *The Wall Street Journal.*

[Approximately 46 words from personal communication by Noam Chomsky with the author, 1991.] CREDIT: Reprinted with the permission of Noam Chomsky.

Connie Bruck, excerpts from *The Predator's Ball* (New York: Penguin, 1988). Copyright © 1988 by Connie Bruck. Reprinted with permission of Simon & Schuster, Inc., and Penguin Books USA.

Susan Trausch, excerpts from "The Generous Greed Machine," *Boston Globe* (March 4, 1990). Copyright © 1990 by the Globe Newspaper Company. Reprinted with the permission of *The Boston Globe.*

Rob Polner, excerpts from "A Real Education in the New York City School System," *In These Times* (April 11–17, 1990). Reprinted with the permission of *In These Times,* a biweekly news magazine published in Chicago.

Excerpt from "Warning: The Standard of Living Is Slipping," *Business Week* (April 20, 1987). Copyright © 1987 by McGraw-Hill, Inc. Reprinted with the permission of *Business Week.*

Phillipe Bourgois, Excerpts from *The New York Times* article. Reprinted with the permission of the author.

Craig Wolf, excerpts from "Ten Teen-Age Girls Held in Upper Broadway Pinprick Attacks," *The New York Times* (November 8, 1989). Copyright © 1989 by The New York Times Company. Reprinted with the permission of *The New York Times.*

Dirk Johnson, excerpts from "In U.S. Parks, Some Seek Retreat, But Find Crime," *The New York Times* (August 21, 1990). Copyright © 1990 by The New York Times Company. Reprinted with the permission of *The New York Times.*

Tom Ashbrook, excerpts from "A View from the East," *The Boston Globe Sunday Magazine* (February 19, 1989). Copyright © 1989 by the Globe Newspaper Company. Reprinted with the permission of *The Boston Globe.*

Phillipe Bourgois, "Just Another Night on Crack Street," *The New York Times* magazine, pages 148-150, April 20, 1987. Copyright © 1987 by The New York Times Company. Reprinted by permission.

Index

Trump, Donald, 3, 15
trust, 118, 119
Tucker, Karla Faye, 112
Tulloch, Robert, 97
Turnbull, Colin, 5–7
Twain, Mark, 36
Tyson Foods, illegal political donations, 84

unemployment, 3
unions
    demonization of, 49, 66
    maquiladora unionization efforts, 72, 87
    resurrection of, 134
    and social contract, 79
    textile mills, 68
United Airlines, employee ownership, 127
United Nations Universal Declaration on
        Human Rights, 131
United Technologies, criminal activity by, 85
Upham, John, 97
upper class, 16
    under Reaganomics, 50
Useem, Michael, 81

Verizon Communications, downsizing, 78
violence, 17
    domestic, 8, 98–99, 134
    and individualism, 12
    in national parks, 97–98
    and oversocialization, 28–30
    state-sponsored, 111–114
    in streets, 92–95
    in suburbs and small towns, 95–97
violent entertainment, 57–58
volunteer work, 13, 134

Waco tragedy, 113
wages, 49
Walk for Hunger, 120
Wall Street
    and corrupted American Dream, 15–16
    economic wilding, 80–83
    financing of global economy, 66
    rewards downsizing companies, 78, 81
    Robin Hood Foundation, 121
Wall Street, 44
Wall Street analysts, as king-makers, 81–82
Wal-Mart
    annual sales, 67
    and Fair Labor Association, 88
Warner-Lambert, criminal activity by, 85
wealth
    concentration in fewer hands, 49
    pressure to pursue, 15
    single-minded pursuit of, 9
Weber, Max, 112
Weirton Steel, employee ownership, 127
Weissman, Robert, 84–85
Weitzman, L. J., 101–102
welfare, 50, 107
Wetzel, James R., 100
whisper numbers, 82
White, Steven, 34
white lies, 9

white wilding, 4
Who Wants to Marry a Multi-Millionaire, 46
Wigand, Jeffery, 84
wilders
    new ethos rewards, 13
    and two Americas, 13–14, 121
    ultimate wilders: killing family for
        money, 3–4, 8, 23–39
wilding
    advertising's influence, 47–48
    causes, 17–20
    civil society as antidote to, 118–119
    on college campuses, 53–56
    cycles of wilding periods alternating with
        civility, 17
    domestic violence, 8, 98–99, 134
    epidemic in America, 7–10
    in everyday life, 41–42
    and family deterioration, 100–102
    famous incidents, 1–5
    forms of, 8–10
    Hollywood's influence, 43–45
    hopeful signs, 119–122
    infrastructure deterioration, 103–105
    kids and money, 56–59
    legitimation, 17
    and new communitarianism, 122–124
    origin of term, 3
    and social market, 124–128
    stopping, 131–135
    and tax revolt, 105–111
    television's influence, 45–47
    two Americas, 13–14, 121
    types of, 10
    violence in national parks, 97–98
    violence in streets, 92–95
    violence in suburbs and small towns,
        95–97
    See also economic wilding; expressive
        wilding; institutional wilding;
        political wilding; social wilding;
        instrumental wilding
wilding culture, 13
    and family, 98
wilding society, 14
Williams, Charles "Andy," 95
Williams, Larry, 51
Wolfe, Alan, 119
Wolfensohn, James, 86
wolfpack, 2
Woodward, Kenneth L., 102
worker ownership, 126–128
workplace rage, 8
World Bank, 86, 88
World Trade Association, 86
World Trade Organization (WTO), 66, 74, 88
    Battle of Seattle, 85–86

YM, 58
youth
    on campuses, 53–56
    expressive wilding, 8
    kids and money, 56–59
    See also children

About the Author

Charles Derber is professor of sociology at Boston College and former director of its graduate program in social economy and social justice. His books include *Corporation Nation: How Corporations Are Taking Over Our Lives and What We Can Do About It* (St. Martin's Press); *The Pursuit of Attention: Power and Ego in Everyday Life,* second edition (Oxford); *Professionals as Workers: Mental Labor in Advanced Capitalism* (G.K. Hall); *Power in the Highest Degree: Professionals and the Rise of a New Mandarin Order* (Oxford); *The Nuclear Seduction: Why the Nuclear Arms Race Doesn't Matter—and What Does* (University of California); and *What's Left: Radical Politics in the Post-Communist Era* (University of Massachusetts).

In addition to his scholarly writing, Derber espouses a public sociology that brings sociological perspectives on key social and political issues to a general audience. He has played an important role in the public debate about globalization, corporate power, a new communitarian economics and democratic politics. He appears frequently on radio and television to talk about his books and contemporary political, economic, and social issues.